T0208289

A Harmonized Heart and Mind

A Little Bit of Me, A Little Bit of You

W. Ralph Mangum

WestBow
PRESS®
A DIVISION OF THOMAS NELSON
& ZONDERVAN

WestBow Press books may be ordered through booksellers or by contacting:

WestBow Press
A Division of Thomas Nelson & Zondervan
1663 Liberty Drive
Bloomington, IN 47403
www.westbowpress.com
1 (866) 928-1240

Because of the dynamic nature of the Internet, any web addresses or
links contained in this book may have changed since publication and
may no longer be valid. The views expressed in this work are solely those
of the author and do not necessarily reflect the views of the publisher,
and the publisher hereby disclaims any responsibility for them.

Any people depicted in stock imagery provided by Getty Images are
models, and such images are being used for illustrative purposes only.
Certain stock imagery © Getty Images.

ISBN: 978-1-9736-6299-0 (sc)
ISBN: 978-1-9736-6300-3 (hc)
ISBN: 978-1-9736-6298-3 (e)

Library of Congress Control Number: 2019906610

Print information available on the last page.

WestBow Press rev. date: 06/05/2019

Contents

Foreword

God gifts writers in various ways. Some are gifted to write novels, poetry, memoirs, or short stories, and the list goes on. God gifted Ralph W. Mangum to write brief, powerful sayings. Some of these sayings are beautiful, but that is not the reason Ralph writes them. He intends them to challenge, encourage, edify, and cheer readers. He seeks to give reasons for people to love one another rather than hate, because hatred leads only to destruction, separation, and other evils. Ralph does not seek to impress others with a political ideology or scholarly concepts. He wants to spread truth and the same love that Jesus manifested in sacrificial death on the cross for us all.

One convenient thing about Ralph's little books is that you don't have to read a chapter or even a full page every time you pick it up. You can read one quote and chew on it all day. By the time the sun sets, you will have digested the morsel of wisdom and, hopefully, applied it to your life. I enjoy Ralph's insight. It moves me, builds me up, and motivates me to go on. You must buy the book and read it. It will make you a better person and a more Christlike Christian.

Dr. Steve Fortosis

No pain, no gain

Teaching children to become dependent and always lean on you as a teacher or parent does not aid in their development. It only teaches them to avoid everything that threatens their comfort or dependence.

Every person's confession must be tested in a fire of affliction. Many will seek to escape through the nearest doorway, but the tests will return again and again until the test at hand is passed. These are the times that try men's souls.

Everyone is tested by the circumstances and environment in which they live. This poses an opportunity to move beyond the present state.

God prepares his prophets by trying them in his fire of afflictions; the afflictions produce fruit, which resides in the prophet. The prophet was selected by God because of his many afflictions. These afflictions provide fuel for godly or divine excellence.

Procrastination

Procrastination is not a friend to successful endeavors, nor can it be, because it lulls one into a state of indecisiveness and kills one's zeal and desire to succeed.

Truth

Truth is often defined by humans by how it is defined in the eyes of others. Everyone is defined by something or someone, and their survival is dependent upon how that something or someone defines them. Every created thing is defined by its creator, which frequently differs from its own definition.

The simple things

The simplest things in life can merely be things on which your perspective has changed from difficult to easy. You no longer see them as they are, but they still exist (Proverbs 3:13).

Water under the bridge

As water flows through pipes, blessed are those who form a conduit for others to travel a path from the ordinary to the extraordinary ways of God and help bring victory to those who believe by faith (Isaiah 41:10).

Wisdom in understanding

The demeanor of a wise man is that of humility, and the key to his wisdom is his understanding that his wisdom is not his own (James 1:5).

Move quickly in the Lord

Those who do the work of the Lord should be prepared to move quickly lest ruin overtake their vision (2 Samuel 15:14).

The sentence against an evil work must be enacted quickly (Ecclesiastes 8:11).

He who is quick to follow the whims of his emotions is not wise (Ecclesiastes 7:9).

A heavy heart

The heart heavy-laden with sin cannot long abide the added weight of Jesus Christ at the door.

Confusion resides in the mind of the confused, but truth is found by those seeking such (Jeremiah 29:13).

All good is divinely inspired, and the Father of Lights will illuminate the darkened heart.

Humans seek the low road and walk in the darkness of ignorance, but the light of God will illuminate the way.

Wisdom is a friend to all who seek understanding—lest failure rule the day.

One can be known for much speaking and miss the last flight out of his place of destruction.

Much teaching can be nonproductive because the teacher only provokes students to anger and reflects no compassion. Such students may vent their rage against the teacher, leaving one with lifelong regret.

A man's closest friend can become his worst enemy if his door is never closed to those who share with others whatever is perceived. Certain matters are better left private.

Everything in a person has an opposing force, the purpose of which is to destroy the primary ruler of the house that you are. The good you do will always be opposed by the bad; your strong arm is opposed by your weaker arm.

Be the victory you seek in your life and the manifestation of the power of almighty God rather than the manifestation of the enemy, whose role is to kill and destroy you (Luke 8:46).

How can a person know one's tendencies unless he has been tempted? How can he know victory unless he has known defeat and is now walking by faith in the promises of God?

Many seek to escape from circumstances but should have a proper place to escape to so they will burst free from their prisons en route to Jesus Christ. They are like those living in a place of confinement, not knowing they actually have the key to their door to freedom.

My biggest challenge in life should be to move to a place higher than my present, but my lack of desire to move to higher ground has me fixed in one place. I'm quite possibly unaware that the way is ever before me.

As a mushroom grows in the dark, so does the opposition to do the will of God in the absence of God's light in the mind (Isaiah 50:10).

As we encourage ourselves and others with uplifting words of hope, we sow seeds of victory in the lives of those who are without hope. Then we will no longer follow our tendency to collapse under the power of pain, defeat, and hopelessness.

In every life, some rain must fall, and a storm is sure to come, but he who sleeps during the storm is not wise lest he sleep his life away (Psalm 83:15).

God will never send you to a place to which he has not prepared a road on which to travel (2 Corinthians 10:16).

The love of God compels many to move slowly and deliberately that they may find him in their searches (Jeremiah 29:13).

Embrace the good, and good will come to you (1 Corinthians 9:11).

When God speaks, and you don't understand, it may well be because you don't like his tone or he's directing you to a place you swore you would never go (Luke 24:25).

God never leaves those who are his for long, though he sometimes hides his face that they may learn by faith a lesson in patience.

A man living in the springtime of his life can profit from mistakes made in the fall. He may then advance in anticipation of a bountiful harvest in the summer, learned from mistakes made in the winter of his discontent (Daniel 2:21).

Today is the culmination of all of one's life experiences, refined through the cross. What we do tomorrow (should we still be here) can be defined by what we do today.

Wisdom generates action not otherwise attainable, for wisdom perpetuates know-how.

Speaking words of knowledge manifests the mind of God in that God knows and the prophet speaks.

There are "words of knowing," which flow from the lips of a godly, ordained man with a prophetic gift.

The divinely appointed prophet is known by God, but any growth of pride comes before his fall.

The Word of God is a burden to those who went half-heartedly and were not selected and a blessing to those who were sent to set the captives free.

Who are the wiser? They who stay to build on what they have, or they who run away to find an ever-fleeting dream?

If you are seriously concerned about your future, even into eternity, you cannot allow your past to define your present, because if you do, you will always manifest your past, and your integrity will be in doubt by all who see you as you always were. God forgives, but you must not cease to fight errant tendencies (Hebrews 8:12).

Avoiding a confrontation may save your life, spare your feelings, or else cause you to miss a chance to grow by overcoming an obstacle. Understand the whole of a matter before you choose.

Assumptions and gossip are two sides of the same coin, but understanding is a distant truth—far off in the minds of those who slander.

Never commit to anything of questionable consequence lest your life become a life of misery.

Know the lay of the land before venturing out of your comfort zone.

A restful night and the peace of God, many seek but few find and possess.

The inevitable you

Everyone's daily walk is on their path toward the ultimate and inevitable destination, at which time they will be judged according to the good they have done in Christ. Have we helped others move up to a better place? Have we inspired and not hindered their growth as persons of value and worth?

In stark contrast, if we allow others to define "right" or "wrong" based on their personal definitions, or allow their likes and dislikes to rule, we will always be defined by or emotionally owned by those persons. Consequently, we are no longer our own as defined by Jesus Christ, Son of the living God.

My right to choose

God has given every man and woman the right and ability to choose anything among the multitude of things created in, above, and beneath the earth and the right to suffer the consequences of the choices we as created beings make in the process of life as measured by time.

If you believe being alone is not best for you, then you must endure the consequences of sharing your life and what it entails. You will no longer be completely alone with God. Hopefully the one of your choosing will always be there to help whenever you stumble into a ditch.

Running to the top (It's their dream)

A man's zeal in running to the top of his chosen profession, even though assumed by some to be entitled, must by necessity in the process of time be reined in by a degree of wisdom and understanding. The zeal, in actuality, is only the means to an end. We must make certain that our zeal is leading to a measurable and constructive goal—one that will stand the test of time.

Godly truth and understanding are divinely orchestrated, but "pride cometh before a fall."

Real beauty

The woman whose beauty originates from within her heart is fully aware of her beauty and need not advertise her attributes to affirm what she already knows. She is affirmed by her humble spirit and love of God manifesting on the outside and her self-confidence, exemplified by the character of Christ, manifested by her inner presence.

Don't worry

Worrying about things you can't fix or understand is always the result of believing you are the beginning and end of what transpires in your life. Consequently there is always a warning just before a storm. However, everyone should be able to discern the warning because there are public or national warnings. So be wise and understand the signs and times relevant to that period.

The darker the room in a house, the more discernible the light, and the presence of God is more evident during the worst storms of our lives.

Help and don't hinder

1. Help someone by living as an example that personal happiness can be achieved by investing the compassion of the same Christ in others by exhibiting hope and love to someone else not like you.

2. Do not dare hinder by promoting negativity, supporting bad behavior, gossip, judging, lying, encouraging the worst in others, or perpetuating violence.

3. Reach beyond the bough when lonely, afraid, homeless, or hungry; reach beyond the bough.

4. So many have been led to believe they can hide forever in the bough of a big oak tree—thoroughly self-sufficient in all aspects of their lives. However, most are at some point in their lives in need of things or people found only beyond the bough.

Consider this

As created people made after the image of God our Creator, we must be aware that our days are numbered (Psalm 139:16), and regardless of our financial wealth in Wall Street investments, political affiliations, ideologies, denominational doctrines, theological titles, and seminary or Bible classes we have attended, this could be the day of our departure, when we arise and fly away.

The Temptations wrote and recorded a song some years ago that became a hit and top seller among many listeners of that day:

"People, get ready, there's a train a-comin'; don't need no baggage, just get on board. All you need is faith to hear the diesels hummin' (Mark 5:34), picking up passengers coast to coast."

When I consider all the spiritual darkness that surrounds us, I am reminded and encouraged by this: "These three remain; faith, hope and love. But the greatest of these is love" (1 Corinthians 13:13 NIV 1984).

Some things too easily assumed

Some things are easily assumed by those quick to justify their own selfishness in lieu of learning to understand the perspective of those unlike themselves. Both sides may lack wisdom and understanding that there are better options than their present lack of love.

Life, love and unfamiliar things

Life is comprised of many amazing and unfamiliar things; the blind see, the deaf hear, and the unschooled gain wisdom and understanding. And yet, those whose occupation requires the ability to see, run against the wind, seeking the fulfillment of a dream on another person whose understanding is his assumption or supposition.

But our love is based on a thing common to all, a desire for love and a desire to love even though we don't know how to give or show it because we've never been loved. Even the consummation of a moment of physical intimacy is not real and satisfying beyond the moment.

Your right and my wrong

Everyone is defined by someone or something, but those who define another based on their perception of "right" and "wrong" has become a god of their own creation. Wisdom and understanding is far off, for their understanding is that of a fool. Your right may be my wrong.

Words of wisdom

How can individuals understand the pain and joy that affect others unless they have lived the life of those who are affected? Their own biases become evident and add to an already darkened environment.

The love of honey cannot determine the life of a queen bee any more than the promises of a greater tomorrow by another human, because both are subject to powers greater than they.

Mere words can help define but not determine the light of day. They can only reveal the content of the heart.

Not all sickness is unto death but can give one pause to consider the content of the heart because the heart's depths are a closed book fully known only by two.

How can we not realize we lack wisdom? We must gain the understanding that we are vain at our best, for we did not self-originate as some believe but are second to the original creator.

A wise man is slow to speak, but his presence is known by many, and the slowness of his speech does not hide the insight of his understanding.

Hatred, jealousy, and envy are another threefold cord not easily broken but by love. These messengers of evil may masquerade as honorable, loving, glad, peaceful, and unified, but their kiss is as deadly as a pit viper.

The love of God cannot be disguised for another, and the light of God cannot be hidden in a dark place—only in the minds of some.

The unknown is frequently revealed in circumstances unplanned or in unfamiliar environments, where doors are opened to blinded eyes.

The good in you will always promote your greater potential, and your wisdom and understanding will demonstrate this if you love people and don't hide this under a rock or in the recesses of your mind.

As laughter promotes laughter, so do love, gladness, happiness, joy and your potential for the same, but a bitter heart is hard to appreciate (Proverbs 3:13).

Befriending a stingy man can be hazardous for lack of a generous friendship.

Greed and stinginess are twins of the same brood of hoarders, and joy is not their friend.

What persons regularly repeat is what they habitually do and learn, and that thing becomes a dominant force in their lives. Example: the good in God we speak can define who we are, but so can the ailment in our bodies.

The wedding band should be an affirmation of the marital contract already anointed by God in a couple's hearts.

The wife of a friend as a lover can be just that: one who kills in a friendly way.

We are each composed of experiences, perceptions, understanding, and how we relate to those things. We cannot truthfully relate to what we have not experienced because of a lack of personal insight.

Every person's mind is at some point in life filled with questions that have answers too complex for us to understand due to our natural but limited perception of life. So wisdom is limited to our natural but limited understanding of ourselves and our tendencies. But our eyes can help us avoid visible harm or deceive us into foolish steps. How can we avoid or find things unseen lest we be guided or directed by the Spirit of God in Christ Jesus, for God is spirit?

Among the many things that can bring joy and happiness into the lives of most people is a spirit (sense) of peace in and around them and those related to or of concern to them.

What is peace? A state of calm and quiet, freedom from disturbing thoughts or emotions. The keys to inner peace begin with the content of the mind: "but be ye transformed by the renewing of your mind" (Romans 12:2 KJV)

1. Don't look for faults in others, because everyone has faults of one kind or another.

2. Seek the company of peaceful people.

3. Don't criticize things you don't understand.

4. Seek the best in others by being an example of the good you don't see in others.

5. Think on the good and not the bad.

6. Avoid conversations that engender strife.

7. Avoid negative-prone people.

8. Avoid blaming or criticizing others.

9. Avoid fretting over things you can't control.

Families don't always agree

Living a productive life becomes easier when persons acquire a degree of wisdom and discretion and acknowledge that they need these attributes in order to live easier, less stressful lives.

Climbing from a place lower than your present place, while trying to rise from an ordinary place to a place of extraordinary potential, will always be opposed by others. This is frequently manifested in those closest to you, such as family and others who have access to your heart.

Frequently your desired new place may not be ideally suited for those who oppose your rise. Again, the strongest opposition can possibly be family members or acquaintances.

"The steeper the hill, the harder the climb, and only the strongest will survive."

Prayer. "Do not be anxious about anything, but in everything by prayer and petition, with thanksgiving, present your requests to God" (Philippians 4:6 NIV 1984).

My sacred circumstances

"All things work together for the good of them that love God" (Romans 8:28).

When I accepted God into my life, I entered a relationship like no other except that of a parent and child. In my life everything is in the hand of God and it is He who orchestrates the circumstances in which I find myself.

God brings things into my life that I cannot at all understand. But the Holy Spirit (the Spirit of God) understands.

God is bringing me into places and circumstances and among people that are right in the palm of God's hand. I can never put my hand in front of my face and say, "This or that is best for me," or "I will do this or that."

This would be an insult to the Lord because I'm saying to him, "You're not capable of taking care of me or guiding my life," or "I know better than you what's best for me; I will determine my goal and destination."

Thus, my joy, happiness derives partly because of those for whom I intercede in prayer. I am here not to judge but to help and not hinder—to take on spiritual assignments given by God.

My end, your end

"How much better to get wisdom from God, to choose understanding rather than silver." The highway of the upright (which is defined by God) avoids evil. "Those who guard their way (their tongue, attitude) guard their lives."

Everyone's daily walk is moving unavoidably toward their ultimate destination, at which time they will be judged according to the light they've been given and the good they have done to help others move up (not down) to a better place, to "help and not hinder" their growth in mind, body, and spirit.

Consequently, we must ignore those who allow another to define "right" or "wrong" based on their personal definition. The likes or dislikes of others will always be defined or emotionally owned by those others. Consequently, we risk being no longer identified by our own character but enslaved by another's.

Everyone is defined by someone or something and is owned by that person or thing. Choose to be defined by the Supernatural Creator of all things: Jesus Christ (see Proverbs 16:16–17).

Where is my hope?

Sooner or later there will come a time when you will see the eternal things that have sustained you in the past during times of emotional or even spiritual darkness, when troubles seemed to come in bunches and hordes of defeatists just seemed to overwhelm you. Even the usual and dependable night of rest seems far off or somewhere in the dim future. But my God says:

Everything written in the past was written to teach us, so that through endurance and the encouragement of the scriptures we might have hope. (Romans 15:4)

You are not alone

No matter your national origin, date of birth, skin color, educational background, political affiliation, or bank balance, you were created for a specific purpose in a specific season, in a specific place, and in a time orchestrated by divine order. And for this reason, God has assigned you an aide and Comforter to guide you along your way if you are his and will accept this in obedience and faith.

Be very careful in this respect because many have "entertained angels unawares" (Hebrews 13:2 KJV). All things are created by a Greater, and the lesser is potentially responsive and responsible to that One Greater.

Some acquaintances are "friends indeed," assigned by divine order (Psalm 91:11–12) to aid and comfort you in your journey through life. Cherish them and they you in love, for they are sent by their God.

It's all up to me

The dictionary defines the word *potential* as "possible" as opposed to "actual."

One can be lovable as opposed to unlovable. I can choose to believe as opposed to distrust, to be gregarious rather than aggressive. Spiritually, "all things are possible for him who can believe" (Mark 9:23).

Among the many aspects of living, I've learned in my quest to "help and not hinder" growth in the life of others over whom God has allowed me influence. My "potential" is frequently far greater than I realize.

In my climb to literal and spiritual places, I have grown through the challenges before me at a given time. But my potential to move forward and "upward" on a "high" road vs. the popular, often-traveled "low" road can be equally challenging.

I soon found out this was not an unusual circumstance in the lives of others, for each of us has the potential to help and not hinder whomever we will; it's only a matter of desire that stems from the heart and not an agenda based on my view of another's worth.

In places of wisdom

The success we often seek is frequently found in a place where wisdom has brought us, but lack of understanding has hidden her face, and our vision dies for lack of understanding caused by an excess of confusion. Sometimes this misunderstanding is caused by well-meaning people whose intentions were to help but who hindered us, resulting in the death of our vision.

Food for thought

Much of what I don't know is an invitation to seek wisdom in learning, but understanding is the key to using what I have already learned.

An arrangement between two people is just that—an arrangement. A relationship may consist of each contributing an understanding of the other's needs; two as one equals unity.

Every naturally occurring element consists of two dissimilar but necessary parts that comprise the same; and the two can be One.

Your new beginning

The beginning or start of something new can be pleasant and exciting. "In the beginning was the Word, and the Word was with God, and the Word was God" (John 1:1).

Many people are enduring some things in their lives that could have been prevented if they had known the potential influence a "new beginning" could have on their past, present, and future. Developing a new way of thinking invariably requires one to move from a place of comfort or familiarity, which can be scary. A "new place" may be a challenge to seek a job in a new place rather than grow stagnant in the same unproductive hometown—it may involve going back to school, meeting new people, finding more ways to love others—something new.

Be careful whom or what you embrace

The term "embrace" can be defined as "enthusiastically accepting, supporting or encouraging someone or something."

Some have enthusiastically embraced demons masquerading as angels of light (2 Corinthians 11:14; Hebrews 13:2). To embrace should mean to enhance, not drag us downhill.

The darker the night

The darker the night, the brighter the light of day. Humanity was not created to waste away in the heat but to labor joyfully in the sunshine. By necessity we need to survive as souls comprised of the basic elements of the ground. After humanity rebelled, we were forced to toil by the sweat of our bodies. As a result, in the process of time our bodies grow weary and worn. Again, in the process of time we become sick with many ailments common among people today.

Consequently, during some long periods of sickness, even as today, many cry out for God to immediately send relief from the debilitating pain.

"The righteous person may have many troubles, but the LORD delivers him from them all" (Psalm 34:19). The darker the night, the brighter the day.

A woman of wisdom

A woman of wisdom is a woman not easily persuaded by visions of self-glamorization and promises of those with dubious backgrounds who habitually prey on women of low self-esteem.

She is a woman of tact, intelligence, inner beauty, and an ability to see beyond the obvious, for she knows where she is headed and has already planned her route and time of arrival.

She is a woman not attracted to men of dubious abilities--those not capable of providing spiritual, moral, and emotional support to a godly woman. God designs that godly, anointed men should marry equally godly women. These women owe no man anything but the love of God and the reliance upon themselves and their God. These indeed are women of wisdom!

Not running against the wind

Our zeal is often motivated by running to the top of our chosen profession, even if some assume that we are not entitled to reach the top. We must, by necessity in the process of time, learn a degree of wisdom and understanding so that our zeal may be based in actuality. We must not be dragged to the depths of failure by others, regardless of the hurts, frustrations, or mental, emotional, and spiritual destruction others attempt in our step-by-step climb to the perceived top of our chosen profession.

Godly truth and understanding is divinely orchestrated, and pride cometh before a fall (Proverbs 16:18).

Many seek a restful night and the peace of God, but few find it because their seeking is in vain; they tire before the race begins. They run hopelessly against the wind.

Trapped

"[I pray] that they will come to their senses and escape from the trap of the devil, who has taken them captive to do his will" (2 Timothy 2:26).

The dictionary defines the words *snare* and *trap* interchangeably, and in practice they both mean the same thing. A common "snare" in the life of followers of Jesus Christ can occur when we choose a mate to satisfy a perceived need for companionship, only to find the desired qualities in the selected one are not present. The results include a feeling of being trapped in a situation from which there is no apparent escape.

The situation is worsened by an inability to admit that a mistake was made in the initial selection, which becomes more evident in the passage of time. Consequently, this relationship can promote and harbor much disharmony and breed an antagonistic spirit in the hearts of all involved and possibly other relatives or social acquaintances.

As in other situations, there is pain and suffering, so it is highly recommended that professional clinical counseling examines the core of the problem that it may be "cauterized," along with much prayer, confession, and repentance. However, it is highly recommended that the most devoted and abandoned workers in Christ administer counseling in such situations. Otherwise, the relationship might suffer irreparable harm when it is already fraught with immeasurable spiritual and emotional tumult, leading to complete disaster.

Two Roads

Every destination has two roads; one for the wise and one or more for the foolish.

Some Things People Ponder What does the Bible say about . . .? Making decisions

He guides the humble in what is right and teaches them His way (Psalm 25:9; 32:8).

Thankfulness

"Give thanks in all circumstances, for this is God's will for you" (1 Thessalonians 5:18).

Of Christ

"Therefore will I divide him a portion with the great, and he shall divide the spoil with the strong; because he hath poured out his soul to death: and he was numbered with the transgressors, and he bare the sin of many, and made intercession for the transgressors" (Isaiah 53:12 KJV).

Grace: enough for all human need

"And He has said to me, 'My grace is sufficient for you, for [my] power is perfected in weakness.' Most gladly, therefore, I will rather boast about my weaknesses, so that the power of Christ may dwell in me" (2 Corinthians 12:9 NASB).

Good for evil

"But love your enemies, do good to them, and lend to them without expecting to get anything back. Then your reward will be great, and you will be children of the Most High, because he is kind to the ungrateful and wicked" (Luke 6:35).

Long life

"Even to your old age and gray hairs I am He. I am He who will sustain you. I have made you and I will carry you; I will sustain you and I will rescue you" (Isaiah 46:4).

Death

"For all men can see that wise men die—the foolish and senseless alike—perish and leave their wealth to others" (Psalm 89:48; Ecclesiastes 3:19).

Stinginess

"He who gives to the poor will lack nothing, but he who closes his eyes to them receives many curses" (Proverbs 28:27).

"I have seen a grievous evil under the sun; wealth hoarded to the harm of the owner" (Ecclesiastes 5:13, Isaiah 23:43).

Generosity

"Be careful not to practice your righteousness in front of others to be seen by them. If you do, you will have no reward from your Father in heaven" (Matthew 6:1).

Tithes

"Bring all the tithes into the storehouse, that there may be food in My house, And try Me now in this," says the LORD of hosts, 'if I will not open for you the windows of heaven and pour out for you such blessing that there will not be room enough to receive it" (Malachi 3:10 NKJV).

Ignorance toward God

"For My people are foolish, they have not known Me. They are silly children, and they have no understanding. They are wise to do evil, but to do good they have no knowledge" (Jeremiah 4:22 NKJV).

Ignorance concerning Jesus Christ

"Jesus answered: 'Don't you know me, Philip, even after I have been among you such a long time? Anyone who has seen me has seen the Father. How can you say, "Show us the Father"?'" (John 14:9).

Spiritual ignorance

"They are darkened in their understanding and separated from the life of God because of the ignorance that is in them due to the hardening of their hearts" (Ephesians 4:18).

Divine knowledge

"Do you not know? Have you not heard? The Lord is the everlasting God, the Creator of the ends of the earth. He will not grow tired or weary, and his understanding no one can fathom. He gives strength to the weary and increases the power of the weak" (Isaiah 40:28–31).

Marriage

"Are you pledged to a woman? Do not seek to be released. Are you free from such a commitment? Do not look for a wife. But if you do marry, you have not sinned; and if a virgin marries, she has not sinned. But those who marry will face many troubles in this life, and I want to spare you this" (1 Corinthians 7:27–28).

"For the husband is the head of the wife as Christ is the head of the church, his body, of which he is the Savior … However, each one of you also must love his wife as he loves himself, and the wife must respect her husband" (Ephesians 5:23, 33).

Satan

"And no wonder! For Satan himself transforms himself into an angel of light. Therefore, it is no great thing if his ministers also transform themselves into ministers of righteousness, whose end will be according to their works (2 Corinthians 11:14–15 NKJV).

Sexuality

"Flee from sexual immorality. All other sins a person commits are outside the body, but whoever sins sexually, sins against their own body. Do you not know that your bodies are temples of the Holy Spirit, who is in you, whom you have received from God? You are not your own; you were bought at a price" (1 Corinthians 6:18–20).

"Or do you not know that wrongdoers will not inherit the kingdom of God? Do not be deceived: Neither the sexually immoral nor idolaters, nor adulterers, nor men who have sex with men, nor thieves, nor the greedy, nor drunkards, nor slanderers, nor swindlers will inherit the kingdom of God. And that is what some of you were. But you were washed, you were sanctified, you were justified in the name of the Lord Jesus Christ and by the Spirit of our God" (1 Corinthians 6:9–11).

The heart stores but the mouth reveals the truth

"You brood of vipers, how can you who are evil say anything good? For the mouth speaks what the heart says, which is full of lies" (Matthew 12:34).

Who are angels?

The word for angels occurs 108 times in the Old Testament and 165 times in the New Testament. The Bible narrative does not present a continuous scenario of angelic activity, but angels do have significant interventions and interactions with one another and with humans.

In thirty-four of its sixty-six books, the Bible writers mention angels—seventeen in the Old Testament and seventeen in the New. The Bible classifies angels as either good or evil. The good are "chosen" (1 Timothy 5:21) and "holy" (Matthew 25:31). They worship and serve God faithfully and energetically (Hebrews 1:7).

Evil angels include Satan, their chief (Matthew 12:24–26), and demons (Matthew 25:41). They oppose God and His servants, human and angelic. These two armies carry on a great battle that surpasses human thought and affects the lives of individuals and nations.

Spiritual Sons

"Let a double portion of thy spirit be upon me."

Like Solomon, Elisha asks for no worldly advantage, but for spiritual power to discharge his office aright. The "double portion" is that which denotes the proportion of a father's property which was the right of an eldest son (Deuteronomy 21:17). Elisha therefore asked for twice as much of Elijah's spirit as should be inherited by any other of the "sons of the prophets." He simply claimed, i.e., to be acknowledged as Elijah's firstborn spiritual son (2 Kings 2:9).

Question: "What does it mean not to give the appearance of evil? (1 Thessalonians 5:22).

Answer: Many Christians assume that to "abstain from all appearance of evil" (1 Thessalonians 5:22 KJV) is to avoid behaviors which anyone might perceive as being wrong. Not only do we flee from that which is evil, we flee from that which *appears* to be evil. For instance, a pastor should not be seen frequenting a bar because someone may think he is getting drunk. However, the actual meaning of this verse is a matter of some debate within Christendom.

Depending on the Bible version you use, 1 Thessalonians 5:22 refers to the "appearance of evil" (KJV), "every kind of evil" (NIV and NLT), or "every form of evil" (NRSV, NKJV, and ESV). Each is a good translation. The Greek word translated "appearance," "form," or "kind" can mean any of these things. The same word is used in 2 Corinthians 5:7 and translated as "sight."

Obviously, the difference in translations can lead to a difference in application. Is it the *appearance* of evil we should be concerned with, or is it staying away from all *forms* of evil?

One problem with emphasizing the *appearance* of evil is that it can make us slaves to the perceptions of others. There will always be someone who thinks that something you are doing is wrong, or that it *looks* wrong to him. So rather than spending our time getting to know God and serving Him, we worry about the possibility that someone, somewhere, might misconstrue our words or actions. In the same letter that he wrote about avoiding evil, Paul wrote, "Just as we have been approved by God to be entrusted with the gospel, so we speak, not to please man, but to please God who tests our hearts" (1 Thessalonians 2:4 ESV). Our goal is to live righteously before God, not to comply with others' arbitrary standards of conduct.

At the same time, we are instructed not to allow our Christian freedom to become a stumbling block to others (1 Corinthians 8:9). We are also instructed to be salt and light in the world (Matthew 5:13–16). Christians have been set apart (2 Corinthians 6:17).

Perhaps looking at the broader context of 1 Thessalonians 5:22 will prove instructive. The verses immediately preceding Paul's exhortation state, "We ask you, brothers, to respect those who labor among you and are over you in the Lord and admonish you, and to esteem them very highly in love because of their work. Be at peace among yourselves. And we urge you, brothers, admonish the idle, encourage the fainthearted, help the weak, be patient with them all. See that no one repays anyone evil for evil, but always seek to do good to one another and to everyone. Rejoice always, pray without ceasing, give thanks in all circumstances; for this is the will of God in Christ Jesus for you. Do not quench the Spirit. Do not despise prophecies, but test everything; hold fast what is good" (1 Thessalonians 5:12–21). This is a quick rundown of how the Thessalonians should be living, "in a manner worthy of God" (1 Thessalonians 2:12).

So what is our conclusion? To avoid the appearance of evil, or every form of evil, means to stay far away from evil. We need not become legalistic regarding what others may perceive to be evil. But we do need to remain cognizant of our witness to the world and of our duty to support fellow believers. We should also be aware of our own tendencies toward sin. Rather than flirting with what could lead us into sin, we avoid evil altogether. It is important not to judge others without first judging our own hearts and motives (Matthew 7:1–5). For instance, one pastor may be perfectly capable of drinking alcohol in moderation and therefore have no problem drinking a bit. Another may be prone to alcoholism or drunkenness and should therefore avoid bars.

Avoiding the appearance of evil, or abstaining from every form of evil, thus means to live in God's light by the power of the Holy Spirit. We "take no part in the unfruitful works of darkness, but instead expose them" (Ephesians 5:11). We worry not about the perceptions of others but about the integrity of our own walk with Christ. When we avoid every kind of evil, we "make no provision for the flesh, to gratify its desires" (Romans 13:14 ESV).

> I the Lord search the heart and examine the mind.
>
> —Jeremiah 17:10

Among the many things in life a human must contend with is an effort to live a life free of discomfort, whether physical or mental.

To this end, we are ever striving to discover some means whereby we can escape everything that denies us control of situations that determine happiness or joy in our lives. Human beings are spirits living in physical bodies of flesh. Consequently, every aspect of a person's life has a spiritual connection and, if problematic, must be spiritually discerned.

Harmony between the heart and mind will always produce joy and a peaceful spirit, which is the result of a clean heart and right attitude. God searches the heart and mind to see if an individual has accepted His invitation to reside spiritually in that person, which will bring harmony between mind and heart.

When experiencing periods of depression, lack of zeal, or times when the mind just seems to have lost its usual determination and the spirit of peace is lost, stop immediately and seek the reason why.

Once the necessary corrections are made through prayerful repentance, everything will become clear. However, never attempt to move on without the witness of the Spirit of peace.

Whoever walks blamelessly will be saved.

—Proverbs 28:18

You ask, "Why doesn't God save me?" Well, it is the will of God that human beings enter a moral relationship with him. He redeemed you, but you may not have entered a personal relationship with him.

You wonder why he does not do this or that. He has already done this or that, but you have not entered a covenant relationship with Him. All the biggest and grandest blessings of God have already been completed, but they are not mine until I step into a covenant relationship with him. He has fulfilled his part of the covenant, but now I must fulfill my end of the agreement.

Waiting for God interminably may simply reflect unbelief and lack of faith in his covenant. This grieves the Holy Spirit because it reveals a lack of faith in the Lord Jesus Christ to keep his Word. It makes his death on the cross of no effect. If I'm waiting for God to do something in me before I trust him, it will never happen because that is not the foundation on which the grace of redemption is based.

It is a matter of faith in God and his salvation plan via his redemption. A faith in God based on my feelings will not suffice and will not satisfy my obligation to be morally related to him in his covenant with human beings. When I am morally related in a covenant relationship with him, the Spirit of peace will witness to it, and my life will adhere to a change brought on by the Spirit of Christ in me.

> It's up to me to do his will and with his mind I can.
>
> I can't rely on someone else to take me by the hand.
>
> As my Father hath sent me, even so send I you.
>
> —John 20:21 (KJV)

Jesus Christ did not say—"Go and save all souls." The salvation of souls is the supernatural work of God. But he did say, "Go and teach; disciple all nations." You cannot make disciples unless you are a disciple yourself.

When Christ's disciples came back from their first mission, they were filled with joy because the devils were subject to them. Then Jesus said, "Do not rejoice in successful service; the great joy is that you are rightly related to me." A missionary is one sent by Jesus Christ as he was sent by God. The missionary did not choose to be a missionary but was chosen by Jesus Christ. The tendency today is to put the inspiration ahead, putting all else in front of us, bringing it out into the open to display our idea of success. In the New Testament the inspiration is found behind us in the Lord Jesus Christ. He and he alone is to be the source of inspiration.

The missionary's goal is to be true to him and carry out his enterprises. Personal attachment to Jesus Christ and his point of view is the most important duty of the missionary and must not be overlooked. In the work of the missionary the great danger is that God's call is effaced by the needs of people until human sympathy absolutely overwhelms the meaning of being sent by Jesus Christ.

We forget that the one great reason underneath all missionary work is not first the elevation of people or their needs, desires, or goals or the education of people, but first and foremost the command of Jesus Christ—"Go ye therefore and teach all nations."

It's not about personalities, glamour, denominations, creeds, or titles, but the will of Him who sent the missionary—Jesus Christ. We give credit to divine wisdom from whom all guidance flows. Not human wisdom.

> A New me in Spite of Myself All my fountains
> are in you.

> —Psalm 87:7

Despite what many believe, God does not alter our natural virtues. He makes us new creatures on the inside. What we must do if we have any desire to be in Christ and have him dwelling in us is to make sure that the outer man conforms to the new man inside.

He lets us know as he transforms the outer natural virtues by the abiding presence of his Holy Spirit. Where sin abounds grace, much more abounds. It is up to us, with his spiritual help, to crucify the old natural man so that the inner spiritual man has free rein. The new inner spiritual man develops his own virtues, which will always conflict with the natural man if we are adamantly opposed to the new life God has placed inside. He will never force himself on anyone, for every individual must be "fully persuaded" in his own mind. It is a matter of the will.

Sadly, many of us stand like sticks in the mud waiting for God to do something he cannot do because that right has been delegated to us by the grace of redemption. In the meantime, we adamantly hold on to our natural virtues while God is desperately trying to get us in touch with the life of Jesus Christ. However, if we would just yield our natural virtues and allow the life of Jesus to activate and manifest in us, we will become lights in many dark corners, and God will be glorified in the highest.

Knowing who I am in Christ, will help me face the dawn. By knowing who I am in Christ reminds me I'm his son.

A Prayer for Deliverance

Speak to your chosen ones this morning.

This morning I offer up praises and thanksgiving for all who are troubled even as I speak. For there are those whose eyes are filled with tears of despair and those whose hearts are filled with dread and terror of what is to come with the morning light.

My God, my creator and my healer, I lift thy name to Jesus on behalf of all those are filled with despair right now in the midst of their Egypt: for the deserted mother and wife of many years who's been told she must fend for herself during times such as this; for the father who is in deep despair over not knowing the whereabouts of his beloved child; for the child whose parents are during divorce, whose future is uncertain, and for whom darkness is ever present.

I pray for the family whose long-established home must be vacated this morning in foreclosure.

I pray for the pastors whose prayers are constant and ever increasing for the saints everywhere.

I pray for the addict whose fight this morning is against the ravages—the need for more cocaine, and whose money and willpower are depleted.

I pray for the business lady whose strength is on the wane because of the lack of trust in Jesus. Daughter, your prayers are heard, and he says, "Trust me, and come unto me, you who are weary and heavy laden."

I pray for the young man in that place in Iraq where it's been said he is safe, but he knows that's not the truth but a statement for public consumption. My God is with you, son, and he will not let you down, although you have not always been a follower of Jesus Christ. He loves you just the same. Take courage, and know that he is God and God alone.

> He chose to be mistreated along with the people of God rather than to enjoy the pleasures of sin for a short time.
>
> —Hebrews 11:25

We delight in letting everyone know how devoted we are to the cause of Christ—our devotion to our church, our testimonies, and telling others of our Christian deeds. None of that matters to Christ and he simply ignores it. Then he subjects us to intense pain, and we say to him, 'Here I am, send me."

This has nothing to do with our personal sanctification but being made broken bread and poured out wine fit for his table. We can never be made into wine if we object to being crushed as grapes. One cannot drink grapes but the wine from the grape after the grape is crushed. If God only uses his fingers to make us broken bread and poured out wine, we may endure it, but when He uses the fingers of someone we dislike or even hate, or circumstances we swore we'd never find ourselves in, we immediately resist, and some of us will doubt our calling.

What kind of circumstances or whose finger has he been using to crush you? If you are still like concrete, angry, bitter, jealous, or still attached to past injustices, your wine will be increasingly bitter and distasteful.

> From that time many of His disciples went back and walked with Him no more.
>
> —John 6:66 (NKJV)

If, in your zeal to preach the gospel of Jesus Christ, you find that many who professed to be with you in the fulfillment of your vision are no longer attracted to your message of the cross, don't grieve over the loss of friends. It was a personal attachment at the beginning, but as the good news of redemption and the agony of Jesus on the cross began to be revealed in detail, many walked away from shame and guilt.

They no longer felt comfortable in your presence as you related your need for a Savior, and immediately, they identified with your plight and felt the need to escape to a place or someone less challenging. Will friends and relatives challenge your "call"? Perhaps! Will you have second thoughts and consider turning back? Jesus asks, "Do you also want to go away?" (John 6:67 NKJV).

Many began to run this race with long, strong strides, but as the hills and dips in the road became more frequent and there were longer intervals between rest stops, their determination became less of a threat to the devil and his opposition stronger, so they slowly stopped competing. "For many are invited, but few are chosen" (Matthew 22:14). Count the cost, and see if you are ready to pay what will be demanded of you (Proverbs 20:25).

> And now I stand so all alone
> for now it's me and thee.
>
> The group has gone their separate ways
> A challenge, just for me.

To be a personal sacrament to God, you must be crushed. Before we can be broken bread and poured out wine, we must be morally related and adjusted to his ways of doing things.

Get right with God and allow him to do as he will; learn of him and his ways; his likes and dislikes. Once you do that, you'll find that he is making you fit for the Master's table: broken bread and poured out wine.

Jesus… led them up a high mountain by themselves.

—Matthew 17:1

Alone with Jesus is like nothing else with which we can identify. We always need a point of reference to enhance our understanding, and if our point of reference is not there, our comprehension is limited to what we have experienced in the past: what we feel, see, hear, or can touch. When God gets us alone by affliction, temptation, sickness, heartbreak, or disappointment in a relationship, and we have no one else, we immediately become awed.

We think of all we've confessed or claimed about our life in God, but now it seems he's turned his back on us. Have we truly been open and honest in our relationship with him before he brought us to this place of despair? Oh, we say we are his and proudly claim to be obedient to his will, but now we are alone with him, face to face with our own personality. Our will can no longer be blamed for our lackadaisical attitude in serving him.

See how Jesus trained the disciples. It was the disciples, not the crowds, who were awed. He constantly spoke to them, but they only understood after they received the Holy Spirit (John 14:26).

The only thing Jesus intends to be clear to you as a follower of his is the way he deals with you personally, so you'll never understand another's perplexities. We think we understand where they are in Christ until God opens our own heart to the stubbornness, pridefulness, and ignorance that the Holy Spirit reveals in us.

Are you truly alone with him now as you go through your own solitude, or are you standing still, caught between two opinions? "Choose you this day whom you will serve."

> When words are many, sin is not absent, but
> he who holds his tongue is wise.
>
> —Proverbs 10:19

One of the attributes of humans is the need to communicate by whatever means at our disposal, of which the use of the tongue is most prominent. Jesus communicated almost exclusively through speech to his disciples and others, although he was clearly able to communicate his thoughts to them through his Spirit: *"revealed it to us by his Spirit"* (1 Corinthians 2:10).

In the daily transactions of commerce and in communication with God through prayer, much is apt to be said in vain or in excess of what is needed to effectively communicate our desires to God.

Remember these scriptures: "Do not be quick with your mouth," and "out of the content of the heart the mouth speaks." Much speaking will almost certainly result at some point in needless repetitions and in what some biblical versions classify as "babbling" (Matthew 6:7). This obviously does not impress the heavenly Father.

"The Lord searches every heart and understands every motive behind the thoughts. If you seek him, he will be found by you."

—1 Chronicles 28:9 (NIV 1984)

To friends I speak so much about
The things I ought not speak.
I never thought of harm it caused
Or how it made me weak.
I often spoke without forethought
And always had my view
Of things I seldom knew about
Or things I wished I knew.

For as he thinketh in his heart, so is he.

—Proverbs 23:7 (KJV)

If the same dilemma I face today is not resolved this day, tomorrow it will have emotionally multiplied, and a resolution will seem less likely. What I assume physically today is what I will assume tomorrow because of the way I have been taught and learned to believe. There are those who believe, "Once a fool, always a fool" and "Once an addict, always an addict," etc.

What I believe is what I invest most of my energy in, and my focus is not on anything that does not coincide with or affirm my belief. If I believe I am still addicted to something, whatever it may be, although all indications are that I am free from that thing, I am still emotionally and mentally addicted.

The same principle applies spiritually. If I have sought divine guidance and believe in my heart that God will provide a solution, it will come. For the disciples of Jesus Christ there are no problems, only challenges and solutions. I am frequently seeking a solution in familiar places and times convenient for me. I seek solutions in my schedule and in ways with which I can readily identify. I must remember that his timing is not my timing, and neither is his method of evaluating my needs. Invariably his solution will come from a direction and source with which I am not familiar. It occurs on his schedule, not necessarily my own. Nevertheless, it is always on time.

Many have learned this biblically sound principle: preparation always precedes blessings, whether the preparation is a stormy life experience or a spiritual high place. Storms purify, classify, separate, and edify. Just know he will come; just be ready yourself to receive him when he does.

> Do you think I came to bring peace on earth? No, I tell you, but division.
>
> —Luke 12:51

I will never say that God is hard and will not agree with anyone who does. God is not hard but exceedingly tender and more so than we can realize. Occasionally, he will demonstrate this by immediately rescuing us from a situation brought on by our own indifference or callousness—a situation that would ordinarily result in immediate death or perhaps physical harm. He gives us the freedom to make bad decisions that we know could result in dire consequences.

No, God is not hard but exceedingly tender and merciful. Sometimes a human cannot get beyond his view of God, as hard as it is, because there is a secret thing he or she will not turn loose, a view being held on to. Until I admit I have done wrong and am willing to change, there is nothing God can do. He has chosen not to take us by force.

As a worker, you must reach people where they are—get to the very root of the hindrance. Otherwise, there will be no healing. Jesus says, "You must," and we answer, "But how can we be?" You can't unless you are given a new spirit (Luke 11:13). If there is no admission of need, there is no rescue!

And You're Seeking

May the LORD, who is good, pardon everyone who sets his heart on seeking God—the LORD, the God of his fathers—even if he is not clean according to the rules of the sanctuary.

—2 Chronicles 30:18–19 (NIV 1984)

What are you seeking? You say, "Nothing." And naturally you are not, but the spirit within you is. There is an inborn need for a relationship with our creator that was not created in a test tube or incubated in a dish of chemicals.

God wants you in a closer relationship with himself rather than simply receiving his gifts. He wants you to get to know him personally. Perhaps we can justifiably say that certain things are accidental, circumstances come and go, but God never gives us anything by accident.

Getting into a relationship with God is the easiest thing in the world. Are you seeking great things for yourself? You may ask God for the baptism in the Holy Spirit, and he does not give it. It is because you have not abandoned yourself to him; there are things you will not do.

He's not concerned for your present perfection but for the ultimate consecration.

He's not concerned about making you happy right now, but getting you rightly related to his Son, Jesus Christ, and that is within your ability to do. It's just a matter of your will.

Are the Small Things Too Big for Me?

Seemeth it a small thing unto you to have
fed upon the good pasture, but ye must
tread down with your feet the residue of
your pasture?

—Ezekiel 34:18 (ASV)

Can God trust you with the big things familiar to you?
We frequently see the manifestation of God's manifold
blessings in the life of others and secretly wonder if they
have some special favor with God wherein he blesses them
in some seemingly, extraordinary way but will not bless you.

The question is, can God first trust you with the small
things you're familiar with in life? It is the small things
God uses to prepare us for the bigger things we will
encounter as we travel along life's pathway toward our
eternal destination in heaven. If I've not proved to him my
perseverance, obedience, and truthfulness, then I must
wrestle before him in prayer for the mastery of that which
I already have. In God there is always a godly process, and
no actions are without godly purpose. Nothing in Christ
is left undone.

I must be proven reliable

Entrust these things to reliable men who will also be qualified to teach others.

—2 Timothy 2:2

As Gold I Am

Yet when I hoped for good, evil came; when I looked for light, then came darkness.

—Job 30:26

God always refines and reshapes those he loves and cherishes. First and foremost, they must be those who have confessed his Son, Jesus Christ. Nothing refines and reveals the dross in a saint like the refining fire of almighty God during darkness.

But he never leaves us alone or allows us to be buffeted more than we can endure. Jesus warned Peter; "Satan wishes to sift you as wheat, but I have prayed for you." As a soldier is refined in combat, so is a saint refined among those who are evil and unrighteous. Even your Christian brothers and sisters can subject you to trials. There will be times of darkness, but stand still, and he will come to you in due season if you just stand and let the refining process run its course.

At times I feel so all alone, especially when
in pain.

But then in moments of quietness, I think
of all I've gained. And then I quickly realize
how much I love my life.

In pain I appreciate the absence of pain, I will endure the
strife.

Beautiful for a Moment in Time

People are like grass that dies away; their
beauty fades as quickly as the beauty of
wildflowers. The grass withers, and the
flowers fall away.

—1 Peter 1:24

Physical beauty is only a passing emotional expression
that is pleasing to the eyes and appeals to the mind but
only lasts for a season and then is gone. As seasons vary
according to lunar cycles, so does physical beauty.

As vapor quickly fades and is no more, so is a man's
appreciation for physical beauty. Blurred lines, pronounced
wrinkles, blotted skin, and sagging muscle tissue soon
replace the image of beauty in the mind's eye. This may
be followed by disdain, contempt, and ugliness in its most
hideous expression. And the hunt for the next object of

sensual appeasement begins anew, and life goes on as before, and the beat goes on!

Beyond Sentimentality

Into your hands I commit my spirit.

—Psalm 31:5

When we come to the Lord, we commit ourselves to the leading and guidance of the Holy Spirit until we see what he is after in preparing us to be poured-out wine and broken bread. Until that eventful moment in our lives, our promise to him is little more than a sentimental journey based on our emotional response to the call of God.

Being a follower of Christ places the disciple in places he or she never envisioned, so when the time of pressing comes as one presses a grape, it brings with it shock, and if that disciple has not learned who he or she is in Christ, disillusionment will follow.

Preparation always precedes the blessings of God. "Weeping may endure for a night, but joy comes in the morning" (Psalm 30:5 NKJV). God uses whomever or whatever he chooses to get the nectar from the grape, and he squeezes with the utmost but exquisite care, for we are no use to him as witnesses of his glory in an injured state.

As those committed to God through the redemption of Jesus Christ, we are free from the condemnation of sin but free also to experience the pain and humiliation he endured in his redemption on the cross.

> Do not be surprised at the painful trial you
> are suffering, as though something strange
> were happening to you.

> —1 Peter 4:12

Poured-out wine and broken bread fit for the Master's table is the ultimate destiny for every follower of Jesus Christ.

But Rise and Stand

> But rise, and stand upon thy feet: for I have
> appeared unto thee for this purpose.

> —Acts 26:16 (KJV)

There are many things in this life that I can fight for or against. And both can offer an opportunity to move forward or backward by the challenges they offer. The challenges I face in my human nature are often not as easy as some other things in life with which I must contend.

It is sometimes an awesome challenge just to "rise," let alone rise and "stand" on my own feet when I am used to looking for others to stand for me as a servant of the Lord's ministry. But when I learned there was a divine purpose—that I had been created for just that purpose—it made my rising up to stand much easier because I, right now, saw a purpose that was greater than my reasoning of why I couldn't stand or, more accurately, why I chose not to stand.

But I had to allow the Spirit of God residing in me to reveal that fact to me. The very thing I fought against eventually became my deliverance in spite of my inborn tendency to resist the will of God. Within my human nature is an automatically activated desire to maintain my "business as usual" attitude toward things godly. But I can do all things with the help of Christ, to the glory of God.

Sometimes I try and do succeed, at times I just don't care one whit. The more I try and don't succeed the more I'm in a fix.

Come, follow me.

—Mark 1:17

Our Lord never challenges a saint beyond his ability to respond in a spiritually enhanced way. As Jesus was stretched wide on the cross, so must a saint be stretched beyond one's ordinary ability to endure. Jesus Christ has counted the cost and paid the price, so the saint is challenged to "follow me."

The conditions that a worker must meet are laid down in Luke 14:26–27 and 33. If a worker is not willing to endure, "he cannot be my disciple." These are principles which demand a sacrifice on the part of the worker. They must be personal sacrifices of self in which the right to choose is exchanged for his right to choose for us.

The eye of God will cauterize with fire every nook and cranny to be filled by himself as he stretches us like a bow in the hands of a hunter with an arrow. Many workers can't go because the cost is too great. They feel they are ordinary workers, and extraordinary is simply a sentimental Bible idea. Never allow your mind to entertain any challenge laid before you by God as sentimental.

> Mold me, Lord, to your will
>
> And never mind my tears.
>
> The tears I shed are nothing new,
>
> I've been this way for years.
>
> Just lead me where I need to be.
>
> I'll kick against the pricks,
>
> But in the end, I'll love you more
>
> Cause now, this sinner's sick.
>
> Carrying his own cross.

—John 19:17

One of the hardest things a worker faces these days because of the proliferation of rampant sin is to carry one's cross, that is, to bear one's burden—usually alone. I am locked into my carnality and have my freedom on my back but never realize I have the key.

I much prefer avoiding the responsibility of my cross when I perceive I can shift the weight over onto someone else. But this is only a perception—a façade, for as the journey nears an end, there must be an accounting for the entire journey of my life, and the cost must be paid.

However, there is everlasting hope. Jesus carried that cross for me, but I must accept that fact and the covenant born of that trip to Golgotha.

I am so blessed to have been spared. That cross He bore and did it just for me.

But I bear a cross each day that often no one sees. I feel the pain, in body and in mind.

Relentless in the heavy load because it's for me, it's mine.

Clothing Yes, But . . .

Rend your heart.

—Joel 2:13

The popular notion of submission to God's will is nothing more than giving a minimal amount of time to a favorite place of worship on some particular day of the week and whatever money my circle of friends thinks appropriate.

I can no more consider yielding my heart to an unseen God than I could give away all the gold I have saved for retirement. All creation is in submission to a higher power and is subject to that point of view. However, everything was made by almighty God and, in its individual way, acknowledges him and the need for his sustenance. Humanity, being the crowning glory of God, was given responsibility to care for every life form with the mind to choose whom he would serve. It is the will of God for every human to be in submission to his will in manifested humility.

> Submit to God and be at peace with him.
> (Job 22:21)

It is God's will that everyone come to the saving knowledge of Jesus Christ. However, it is every human's choice whom they will serve and to whom they will submit. Submit to God, be at peace with Him, and see the salvation of the Lord. Any other point of view will grieve the Holy Spirit and not be productive to you.

> You women who are so complacent, rise up
> and listen to me.

> —Isaiah 32:9

It's hard to be elevated when being elevated is not part of your personal character. When the external things in life call on you to "rise up," you may rise up on that occasion to meet the demands of the moment. But elevation is what helps us rise above the ordinary, and God will continually say: "Rise up and listen to me." Then when you get higher, you face other demands that you rise up.

Now Satan often uses strategies to demand you to "rise up" in self-exaltation, pride, and ultimately destruction. Satan uses our common sense and everyday circumstances to tempt us to rise up and experience all the high places in this earthly kingdom: money, fame, adulation, earthly affirmation, etc.

Should we accept God's challenge to rise up, he offers us elevation but to a much higher plane, accompanied by all the glories in his kingdom, all within the hands of almighty God. When the devil places you in a high place, he may denounce your view of holiness for an easier (according to him) road to fame and fortune.

God grants you his grace as you ascend to heavenly places. But first be a ruler over small things, and then he will make you ruler over many (see Matthew 25:21). Someday you may rule worlds without end, and spiritual fame and fortune will be yours in the bonds of humility.

> Come to me, all you who are weary and burdened, and I will give you rest.
>
> —Matthew 11:28

Whatever the circumstances may be in my life, God has advised me even before troubles come my way, "Come to me, all you who are weary and burdened, and I will give you rest." There is no easier thing to do. God desires I do this without hesitation. No further counsel is required; no need to consult with my pastor, my psychologist, or my closest friend. What comes into my mind when I think about God is the most important thing about me. Do I immediately think of God as my personal healer, my deliverer, as the sovereign God, all-knowing, all-seeing, all-powerful?

I had to learn that God is not like me, and my tendency to reduce Him to measurable and controllable terms does not make for a valid view of who he is and what he is to me. He longs for me to see him and to know him, and in his quest for me to move from knowing him vaguely to knowing him vividly, he is willing to take on my heavy burdens and heal me of all my infirmities.

> So I say to you: Ask and it will be given to you; seek and you will find; knock and the door will be opened to you. (Luke 11:9).

> Casting down arguments and every high thing that exalts itself against the knowledge of God.

> —2 Corinthians 10:5 (NKJV)

I must have a made-up mind to be delivered from things. Deliverance from sin is not deliverance from human nature. There are some things in my nature that I must destroy by not participating in their growth—by not revisiting them, reliving them, or glorifying them. Neglect things such as prejudices, gossiping, talebearing, and, for some, deliberately displaying one's physical attributes with the intention of exciting physical arousal in another.

Then there are other things which must be destroyed by the violence of divine strength imparted by the Spirit of God. Then there are things which I should not fight against but stand and see the salvation of the Lord. Every theory, estimation, or conception which erects itself against the knowledge of the living God is to be adamantly destroyed, not by soft-pedaling or nullifying the effect of God's Word with half-truths but by utilizing the power of God.

God must change my disposition before I can enter into a sanctification mode or experience sanctification. In the arena of sin is where the fight begins, but I can never fight against sin and win. Jesus Christ did that in redemption. What I need to do is assume the right, willing attitude and God will do the rest.

"Let that mind be in you which was in Christ Jesus." Wow, I can do that!

Divine Circumstances

And we know that all things work together
for the good of those who love the Lord.

—Romans 8:28

It is only those who are truly abandoned to Jesus Christ who believe that God orchestrates their circumstances. We have endless rationales for explaining our circumstances. We say we believe he engineers our circumstances, but we really do not. We prefer to believe they are engineered by humans because we as mortals are more comfortable rationalizing circumstances engineered by men rather than a supernatural spiritual God, whom we cannot touch, feel, or see.

Then suddenly God breaks up a set of circumstances, and we realize we have been disloyal to him by not recognizing his presence all the while. We never saw what it was he was after—that we need to worship Him in trying circumstances just as in mundane, everyday circumstances.

Many Christians are intensely impatient about speaking of loyalty to Jesus. God is dethroned more emphatically by Christian workers than by the world. The idea is not that we work for God but that we are loyal to him in every circumstance. He wants to do his work through us. "In all thy ways acknowledge him, and he shall direct thy paths" (Proverbs 3:6 KJV).

Do I Really Know God?

If you love Me, keep My commandments.

—John 14:15 (NKJV)

I don't deliberately disobey God; but because I don't respect and honor him, I simply pay him no attention. Sure, I know what he says about this and that. But I know him only by reputation and according to what others have said about him. So I have no personal respect for him. I may not be willfully disobedient but am ignorant because I prefer my own agendas. "If you love me, you will keep my commandments" (John 14:15 NASB). If we do, then we will fully realize how disrespectful we've been, and we may be covered in shame.

Some pray, "Speak to me, Lord," but we really don't want him to speak to us. We may be willing to hear his servants instead. We like to listen to personal testimonies which satisfy a sentimental longing to hear a word about God. But we don't want to hear from God because our sinful nature will not allow us to admit that we're desolate and needy for the presence of God in our life.

Am I putting God in a position of having to treat me as a child because I have been ignoring him? Then when I do hear him, he brings back to my mind the times of disobedience and arrogance in my refusal to obey. "[They] said to Moses, 'Speak to us yourself and we will listen.

But do not have God speak to us or we will die'" (Exodus 20:19).

Do Not Quench the Spirit of God

Quench not the Spirit.

—1 Thessalonians 5:19 (KJV)

Many circumstances arise in the lives of those who profess to love the Lord, and in the midst of some there is a tendency to quench the Spirit of God. Do not quench the Spirit of God; it is very easy to do. We faint when we are rebuked by him and then sometimes hearken back and say, "Well, years ago I was saved, and ..."

If you are morally abandoned to Jesus Christ, there is no need to look back to where you were years ago. If you are walking in the light, there is no fixation on the past. There is nothing wrong with rejoicing in God's past influence in your life. However, the past should be transfused into the present communion with him. Otherwise you may become a sentimental Christian trying to recapture a rapture lost along the way, while he is trying to bring you back into harmony with himself in the present.

If we have only a shallow experience of sanctification, we mistake the shallow for reality, and when he rebukes us, our response is "That's the devil" or "Somebody is after me," or we refuse to see what it is he is after and become adamant in our refusal to accept his rebuke.

If God brings you into a crisis, and you refuse to go all the way through with the right point of view, he will bring it back to you again, and it will not be as easily discerned as before, and the humiliation will be more severe. But if you go through and endure the rebuke, there will be praise to God like never before. When God rebukes you, let him have his way. Let him rightly relate you to himself. Are you prepared to let him grasp you in the palm of his hand and do a work in you that makes you worthy of being poured out wine and broken bread fit for the Master's table? He has to get you in the mind-set and attitude to make you whole by his spiritual revival.

Have You Met Jesus?

While the man was on his way, some of his servants met him.

—John 4:51 (NLT)

If you don't recall ever meeting Jesus or the circumstances surrounding your meeting him, perhaps you have never met him. Many people have met him in some very strange places at odd times. But where you met him is not as important as having met him face to face. The circumstances through which you met Jesus will most likely influence your life and the lives of others around you forever.

Perhaps you met him while you were on your way to Jordan, hoping to hitch a ride over Jordan and up to Bethel.

Perhaps you decided that going up to Bethel with a friend or a mate and crossing over Jordan without getting your feet wet was a far better deal than crossing dirty Jordan. But if you never crossed Jordan God's way, it is safe to say you never met Jesus, because in the thick of the muck and mire, the valley of despair is where you will often meet Jesus because your pride will finally be broken. Just be prepared to meet him whenever he shows up, because he will come sooner or later.

Don't Be a Fool

A human without wisdom and understanding is living on the promises of others whose aim is not in his or her best interest.

An empty can and the mind of a fool have this in common: both are subject to winds of doctrines or perversity.

All fools are subject to the mind of a fool and are apt to become as one. A wise man they will not follow, but only another fool.

A fool is a threat to many and a danger to some, and his mouth will reveal the matter.

The mind of a fool is couched in foolery; though his words are soft, his intentions are soon revealed.

A foolish man and the mind of an amorous woman on the prowl can work as one until the morning light.

Women, if a man is a gentleman, talk to him. If he is neatly dressed, entertain him. If he is rich, get his phone number. If he is gainfully employed, call him. But if he is a fool, run quickly from him, for he will throw you both under the bus.

If your spouse is a fool now, he or she was a fool when you married them. The nuptial clouds you saw over the head as you placed the ring on the finger were distant storm clouds of things to come.

The fool who falls in love will stumble until the divorce decree is final.

Poor fool am I and vain at best. I believe what all you say,

I've never thought to check to see If what you claim will work for me.

God Will Provide

I have learned, in whatsoever state I am, therein to be content.

—Philippians 4:11 (KJV)

Paul didn't say to grumble or complain about the lack of recognition, acknowledgment, or five-star services usually reserved for those whose names are widely known. Nor was he referring to those whose piety has labeled and identified them as holy men and women of God.

The apostle had learned through many trials and tribulations that God would supply all his needs, so consequently there was no gain in despairing about circumstances over which He had no control. But God out of grace has afforded those he's set aside for times such as these that he will supply all their needs according to his riches.

Paul's mental imagery was filled with his knowledge of the will of God in his life because he had established a personal and intimate relationship with the heavenly Father prior to coming to a place of lack and hardship. He had been thoroughly instructed by the Spirit of God and natural circumstances in how to prepare for and maintain himself and his mental attitude when suffering lack. He had learned to look for, appropriate, and appreciate the good in every circumstance in which he found himself.

Every saint and especially those of the cloth will find themselves in circumstances not unlike those which Paul endured for a season. Circumstances try men's souls. Unless you enter into circumstances and endure them as a strong soldier for the Lord until the end, God may send them again until he finds that attribute in you that he's after, and that is for your greater good in Christ Jesus.

Oh, help me, God, to be prepared when evil comes my way or when your hand descends on me just when I need to pray.

God's Retribution of Love

Then you will understand the fear of the
LORD.

—Proverbs 2:5 (NIV)

Understanding gives me a preview of what my God
is capable of: retribution, blessings, and much more. I
understand that the wrath of God is retribution to chasten
me for sins and teach me not to repeat the same sins
again. The wisdom is in understanding and in obedience.
Thus, the love of God is manifested in his retribution and
received as a blessing by me, the sinner.

The Gospel in the Checkout Lane

A fool gives full vent to his anger, but a wise
man keeps himself under control.

—Proverbs 29:11

It's the checkout lane, and you are next in line and this
obnoxious individual boldly elbows herself around and in
front of you. Immediately, your cheeks redden with anger,
and you're about to give her what you know she needs to
hear just from you. You believe you have the answer to her
arrogant, selfish attitude!

Don't do it!

Be humble and gentle. Be patient with each other, making allowance for each other's faults.

—Ephesians 4:2

Shallow Waters Can Run Deep

Guard your thoughts. Don't allow yourself to imagine that God doesn't allow shallow things in your life because they can be just as meaningful as the deep things. It's not your devotion to God that makes you refuse to appear shallow, but your desire to impress others with your "deep" understanding of God, which indicates you are overly pious.

Understanding the depth of God's character begins with being shallow, not judging others for what you deem as shallow. The shallow things of life: eating, drinking, walking, talking, and running are all ordained by God. Jesus came here as a baby. All the things deemed shallow Jesus lived and experienced. He was thirty years old before he began doing and saying things that were "spiritually deep." Spiritual growth for us begins in a shallow understanding of the mind of God and gradually grows up into a deeper understanding—the wisdom of God from God.

The snare is remaining shallow with no obvious movement toward a greater depth and higher heights in Jesus Christ. However, the biggest fraud you'll ever encounter as you seek to impress others with your glorious spirituality is yourself.

> The day God visits you has come ... Now is
> the time of their confusion.
>
> —Micah 7:4 (NIV)

His presence is ever with us, for he visits all his creation every hour of the day. His presence is felt in the billowing gales of the arctic during its cold winter days. His presence is found during the hot, humid days of summer. His presence was in the midst of the hurricanes that battered New Orleans a few years ago. In springtime when his creatures are arising from their winter's sleep to sprout as new creations, he created food for such starving creatures. His presence is manifested in many ways for many reasons, but his love for his creation is paramount, for he did say it was very good!

I never thought of God this way, How vast his presence is,

Or how he's always on the Move, for all he made is his.

Testing Every Spirit

Dear friends, do not believe every spirit, but
test the spirits to see whether they are from
God, because many false prophets have
gone out into the world.

—1 John 4:1

If you believe God has told you to do something, ask him to
confirm it to you three times: through his Word, through
circumstances, and through other people who may know
nothing of the situation. We use our good sense in hearing
God, but we also ask others to use their good sense for
our good. No man or woman is an island, though we are
much more than the sum of our relationships to others.
Those relationships must rest on our personal relationship
to God himself. When *both* relationships are right, we find
perfect safety and full and perfect peace.

Do you commonly "test every spirit," or do you just do the
"smart" thing or call a few friends and do whatever they
advise? Be brutally honest. Ask God to show you what you
would do if you chose to "test every spirit" more diligently.

And, behold, the LORD passed by, and a
great and strong wind rent the mountains,
and brake in pieces the rocks before the

LORD; but the LORD was not in the wind:
and after the wind an earthquake; but the
LORD was not in the earthquake: and after
the earthquake a fire; but the LORD was not
in the fire: and after the fire a still small
voice.

—1 Kings 19:11–12 (KJV)

God may occasionally address us in dreams, visions, and
voices as well as through the Bible and extraordinary
events. Such things are well documented in biblical and
personal accounts. The *significance* of these ways can
confuse us, however. For example, the still, small voice is so
humble that it may be ignored or even discounted by some
who think that only the more dramatic communications
can be authentic. If this view is accepted, a *life* of hearing
God must be filled with constant fireworks from heaven,
which is not reasonable. Rather the still, small voice is one
of God's primary ways of addressing us.

Close your eyes and put yourself in the place of Elijah.
Tense up as the strong wind creates havoc. Brace yourself
as the ground under your feet keeps shifting. Feel the heat
of the fire, and see yourself moving away from it. Then
perk up to the still, small voice.

What does God want to say to you today?

Even in darkness light dawns for the upright.

—Psalm 112:4

The challenge for the follower of Jesus is the willingness to stand up while in the middle of a dark place. Our natural inclination is to escape the rigors of hardship when there is no apparent relief in sight. Every follower of Jesus will be tested, but the promises of almighty God give those who can believe the assurance that, no matter the circumstances, he is ever present, even in the midst of your darkest hour:

"He will never leave you nor forsake you."

(Deuteronomy 31:8)

We immediately pray and look for quick deliverance from our dilemma; but God does not deliver us *from* our circumstances, He delivers us *in* our circumstances.

There is the potential for great growth in our circumstances which we would not otherwise experience if we were immediately delivered from them. Deliverance in spite of our circumstances can be manifested as healing in a dark place.

Never ask God to deliver you from circumstances, but pray for grace to endure this darkness. Rest assured that this period of darkness will only last for a season; "weeping may endure for a night, but joy cometh in the morning" (Psalm 30:5).

Help me, God, to know the truth That light will show the way, That I will have the will to stand And always kneel to pray.

Lord, show us the Father.

—John 14:8

I know that in me there is nothing to brag about, but in the Father, manifested through his Son, Jesus Christ, there is hope. There is hope that far exceeds the ravages of sin in my mortal body. From my mother's womb came I into a sin-ravaged environment as dark as the darkness that held me captive in my mother's womb for nine months.

Show me all that so easily entangles me that I may have a deeper appreciation of the riches awaiting those whose hope in built on nothing less that Jesus' blood and righteousness. So show me eternity that I may look over into that promised land, where exists no pain or suffering and God will wipe away all tears.

Thank you, Jesus, for showing me thy Father on that day so long ago when you met me on the banks of River Jordan, as I cried in the pain of rejection, depression, loneliness, doubt, and fear of all kinds. Those times when I ran although no one was chasing me. I was trying to endure severe chest pains, and church people accused me of things I did not do. I had no friends, and you took me in. Yes, I have met you on many occasions since that fateful day years ago.

Now I thank you for all the things that befall me in my suffering, for in my weakness you are strong.

I've traveled many miles, it seems,

And experienced many things.

Some things I know and understand,

But there are things unseen.

I've often said, I have to see

Or touch the things I hear.

Invisible the spirit world,

And yet I know it's real.

I've seen my Lord and didn't know

Because I could not feel.

Being justified freely by his grace ...

—Romans 3:24

The gospel of the grace of God creates a longing in me and an equal resentment because of what the gospel of Jesus Christ has revealed in me. And that is not acceptable. There is a part of me that will agree and give much, but to accept humbling is a much different thing. I will give myself in consecration, but do not humiliate me to the level of being a liar, a cheater, unfruitful, and deserving of hell. These things I will not willingly accept. My pride will not allow it. Then tell me all I have to do is accept the gift of salvation through Jesus Christ. We must realize we can't earn or win anything from God; we must receive it as a gift or do without it. The greatest spiritual blessing is the knowledge that we are destitute, and until we get there, our God is powerless.

My Life

I despise my life; I would not live forever.
Let me alone; my days have no meaning.

—Job 7:16

I despise my life at times because there are challenges I'm afraid to face. I have been in this deep valley of helplessness for so long, and my enemy is even in the house of God. They are there, deeply entrenched in the halls of righteousness, but their righteousness is not that righteousness that leads to eternal blessedness.

I see them for who they are, but I am stymied in ignorance, shamed by my vulnerability to their wicked schemes. So let me alone. My days have no meaning, and I can't see the light for the darkness that surrounds me. I know of that light because I have seen what I know and knew then was the manifestation of that light. But I cannot reach beyond the darkness that holds me bound. So leave me alone *not*! For the God who created me sees my plight and will deliver me in due season. No, do not leave me alone!

I will remember the deeds.

—Psalm 77:11

The people we remember, those who influence us most, are not the people who constantly challenge us about godly things or about our attitude, but those who live their lives like the stars in the heavens: simple, uncomplicated, honest, and unashamed.

These are the people that mold us. If you want to be used of God, get rightly related to Jesus Christ in the simple, everyday manifestation of his presence in your life, and he'll use you unconsciously every minute of the day, wherever you happen to be.

Redeemed as a Witness

He came as a witness to testify concerning that light, so that through him all might believe.

—John 1:7

Woe to me if I come in another fashion than as a witness of him who saved me for just such a purpose as this. I am wonderfully saved, set aside, a peculiar person, broken bread fit for the Master's table. I am a product of his mind, a manifestation of his handiwork and created after his own image in the likeness of his Son, Jesus Christ.

I am a manifestation of his redemption, a witness of his saving grace, an everlasting presence in the souls of humanity. His Spirit bears witness to the glory of God in Christ Jesus. Woe to me if I serve any God other than him who sent me as a witness to his divine will in Christ Jesus to the glory of God.

Then said Jesus unto the twelve, Will ye also
go away?

—John 6:67 (KJV)

What is your will in this matter? Why did you agree to
be here? What did you expect to see? We will agree with
almost anything that promises excitement, monetary gain,
or some sort of instant gratification. But you say in your
heart, "Do not expect me to agree with you on the grounds
of moral deficiency or to agree with you that I need a
Savior."

You may agree with me that there are things you can
do better: stop cheating on the wife, pay more taxes, be
a better person, give a dollar to the homeless because
these suggestions only promote your own self-image. But
needing a Savior? No way!

Unless the Spirit of God is able to convince me to recognize
the need in me for a Savior, I will not stay. Until I allow the
spirit man within me to have free rein, I'll continue to be
held hostage by the laws of sin. No, I will not stay!

If you love me, you will keep my
commandments.

—John 14:15

Keeping the commandments of our God is always an
option we as free and willing thinkers have at our disposal.
Jesus never said to his followers "Thou shalt" do this or

"Thou shalt not." If we obey him, we do so out of love for him and his truth.

The words he speaks are resonant with the needs of every man, woman, and child but are in opposition to our natural instinct to follow our own understanding of the way things "ought to be." God does not give us rules, but he does make his standards very clear, and if I love him, I will have no problem being obedient to his will in my life for me. If I hesitate in following his will for me, it is because I love something else more than him. When we obey him, we do so out of oneness of spirit with him. He will not push me to obey him; I do that of my own free will and by a personal choice.

When I entertain a view of God in a lopsided, on-and-off attitude based in part on a shallow belief in his divinity, my relationship with him will only be as deep as my devotion to him as the only true and living God. When I give up my right to myself based on his redemption of me and accept his redemption of me for my life, I will be better able to see him as he is. If I obey Jesus Christ, the redemption of God will come forward through me into the lives of others: family, friends, and acquaintances. But the Spirit of God will be the determining factor.

> But blessing crowns him who is willing to
> sell.

—Proverbs 11:26 (NIV 1984)

There exists in every man, woman, and child an innate potential to create and succeed in whatever endeavor he or she chooses to pursue. In the adult this ability is resident and available, but we must be willing to look deep within ourselves, to see beyond our ordinary, mundane circumstances, and must be hungry enough to believe that we will attain goals beyond the familiar "I can't": *I can't do this, I can't do that!*

In a child this innate ability is resident but must be nurtured and cultivated in an environment of love and positive attitudes, or that innate ability will die from lack of proper attention. How does one get to or arrive at a starting point where that innate ability is recognized? That starting point depends on one's past experiences and desire to excel. Hunger is a strong craving or urgent need for food which the body needs to survive; and when this craving is paired with a dream of better things in life, success will follow because now it is a matter of survival.

It all begins with a dream, which is the mind's way of saying, "Go higher." How hungry are you? Are you only mildly "lunchy" with just a passing thought of some past enjoyable moments over a favorite cupcake? Or are you like me—always on the lookout for that better sustenance, that just-right bowl of black-eyed peas?

> Immediately he received his sight and followed Jesus, praising God. When all the people saw it, they also praised God.

> —Luke 18:43

Immediate is an action word that demands a *right now* response, not tomorrow or an hour from now. Many followers of Christ either fall away from following him and advertise him as being a liar or decide that he is an ancient fable created by the ruling classes to enslave the poor.

But everything, every word spoken by our God, every healing performed by him, is always performed immediately unless he wishes it to be gradual! It is blasphemous to accuse the Creator of heaven and earth of being incapable of doing anything like speaking creation into reality. It is we who are the culprits by our lack of faith and our love of darkness more than light. Never accuse the King of glory of not doing what you will not allow.

Immediately

Consider God's wonders.

—Job 37:14

Consider the vast, far-ranging changes occurring globally in governmental entities and in the lives of individuals. Those who know the sovereignty of God can discern immediate or pending changes in their own lives.

If you are one of countless thousands who have prayed through many tear-filled nights seeking divine guidance for things that seemed too complex and painful to handle, be advised that this was a season of spiritual reconciliation. The fact that a spiritual change is at hand is frequently manifested in physical, audible, and visible ways that are discernible to everyone except those who adamantly refuse to see the obvious.

If you discern a "newness" in your spirit, a renewed urgency in your desire to accomplish something you've prayed or fasted for, offer up thanksgiving while acknowledging the One who responded to your need in ways you may or may not understand now. He who is to be destroyed will be destroyed, and he that is to be built up will be built up, and no human can successfully intervene. God has reserved many of his own for times such as this. All promises in Jesus Christ are "Yes" and "Amen."

If therefore thou art offering thy gift at the altar, and there rememberest that thy brother hath aught against thee, leave there thy gift before the altar, and go thy way.

—Matthew 5:23–24 (ASV)

The snare of having the Spirit reveal the imperfection in my understanding of the gospels of Jesus Christ can be disappointing to an avid worker for the Lord. The process of overcoming is a constant revelation of the truths of almighty God. The process also reveals how imperfect I am in and of myself and how much I need the indwelling Spirit of God at work in my life.

"Leave there thy gift before the altar, and go thy way." Do not attempt to offer up to God anything that hints of jealousy, pride, or deceit; the reality of Jesus Christ cannot be uplifted by even the slightest hint of resentment.

The "go and be reconciled" to your brother is to allow the Spirit to search the width and depth of that thing in you. Never quench the work of the Holy Spirit by attempting to stand in the way of what Christ is trying to do through you, because you will be the worse off if you do.

> But a woman who fears the LORD is to be praised.
>
> —Proverbs 31:30

Beware of the tendency to withhold due praise when encouraging words and actions are appropriate, for this also honors our Lord. The woman is unique in her disposition and this uniqueness is manifest in many ways, all to the glory of almighty God who created all things well. Because of her uniqueness, beauty, and charm, she can be a snare to many who are easily seduced by her beauty.

If she is indeed a godly woman, reward her according to her work. Hold not her reward according to your agenda, for she is a godly woman worthy of praise according to the riches of our heavenly Father. As the weaker vessel, uphold and support her in her endeavors to worship Jesus Christ.

> Of a truth I perceive that God is no respecter of persons. (Acts 10:34)
>
> I will pour out my Spirit on all people ... Even on my servants, both men and women;

I will pour out my Spirit. (Joel 2:28–29; Acts 2:17–18)

In all things let us be godly, putting on the whole armor of God. Let all we do be praiseworthy to the glory of God in Christ Jesus.

> Without warning, a furious storm came up on the lake.
>
> —Matthew 8:24 (NIV 1984)

As one who likes to believe that I am fairly up-to-date regarding current events both locally and otherwise, I have found that, unlike past years, every day now seems to bring even more violence than the day before. With this in mind I find myself asking some pretty (from my perspective) hard-hitting questions about my view of the spiritual condition. I am asking who I am in Christ or otherwise.

Despite all the blessings that come in many ways, have I become arrogant and unconcerned about the things of God that directly or remotely relate to me? When storms come my way, will I be able to weather the violent waves as they beat against the very things I value most: spouse, automobile, bank account, job, children, sickness, and finally my own mind?

Will I be able or qualified to mentor my family members in the elements of holiness (Hebrews 12:10) so that they will be able to stand the trial of their faith? Am I an example of what God expects of a godly husband?

Rest assured, storms will come and, in some cases, have arrived already. Perhaps we're seeing only the first and early stages before the terrible gusts. The gusts of extremely violent and unexpected mayhem may begin occurring in even serene neighborhoods. Even the church buildings are not exempt (Matthew 24:6–13). And there is so much more! I have arrived at one conclusion: The Word of God is sure and true to the last comma. And as for me and my house, we will serve the Lord, for the days of the storms are at hand (Luke 17:27–30).

> In the valley of decision! For the day of the
> Lord is near.
>
> —Joel 3:14

I make decisions every day of my life and that's where the rubber meets the road. If the decisions I make determine and affect the outcome of my life only, then selfishness would not be a factor in the decisions I make. Every decision I make can either lead me and others deeper into a valley of desperation or propel me upward into the light, for valleys are usually devoid of light because of the depth. Every decision has weight and is a precursor to another decision. Think it through in anticipation of what is to follow.

Today—right now, not presently, but immediately I decide to make my exit my destination and as it becomes clearly defined, I realize I am heaven-bound, in the light.

Launch Out Into the Deep

"…into the deep …"

—Jonah 2:3 (KJV)

The common attitude of most novice Christians and many mature saints is one of not believing that almighty God would allow them to be placed in a pit of despair. Our understanding of divinity only allows for continuous experiences of creature comforts—never a battle in the depths where growth is matured and then built up into the lives of others.

Natural life consists of a series of antagonistic experiences. One must be declared worthy by the grace of almighty God to enter into the presence of a holy, righteous God, which is opposed by my carnal nature and the world around me. Do not think it strange when the fiery darts of oppression, depression, family hostilities, and at times the very legal system many of us have sworn to protect with our lives find you guilty of some sort of offense.

However, where sin abounds, grace much more abounds. The Word of God declares: the race is not given to the swift nor the battle to the strong, but to him who holds on until the end. God is correcting the rebellion in you so you can launch out into the depths of stormy seas with faith and maturity.

> Eat, because it was set aside for you for this occasion.

> —1 Samuel 9:24

Petitioning God through our prayers is a normal godly expectation by God of those whom he has set aside for his divine purposes. When he has arranged a feast in the middle of a spiritually famished land and in the very presence of our enemies, we must not decline the invitation. If we do, we grieve the Holy Spirit by indicating we have better things to do, and his invitation is not one of priority.

His invitation is personal in that it is in response to your need for divine intervention concerning you and your dilemma, so he has bidden you to come and feast: "This meat was set aside just for you." Come from your dilemma and rest for a season and feast while you rest, for he is not delivering you out of your dilemma but in your dilemma. Come dine and fellowship with me, and I will further encourage you there.

The promises of God are "Yes" and in Christ "Amen," so your invitation is genuine and should not be postponed or denied because you'll regret it for a long time to come. Responses to our prayers often come in strange and unfamiliar ways. Even in the barber chair he might show up. Just be prepared to receive him when he comes, and when he does come, acknowledge him, and in due season he will give you further directions if you faint not, but hold on to his promise, "I will never leave you or forsake you."

Come up hither, and I will show thee things.

—Revelation 4:1 (KJV)

In the ordinary external matters you face daily, you will always be challenged to "come up." If you accept the challenge, you will see things you have never seen before—things you've dreamed of, perhaps, but never seen before. Every chapter in the life of workers is a divine invitation to come up from the ordinary unto the extraordinary—to move from unfamiliar circumstances to a place where learning will continue.

There we will be shown other avenues on which we must travel to attain our highest potential in life. Every worker must experience externally motivated things in life which, if left unchecked, can potentially devastate one's mind, body, and spirit. There is no way to avoid these circumstances as long as one is physically alive.

Come up in your awareness of your dangerous surroundings—in your knowledge of close but jealous and deceitful acquaintances. Come up in the knowledge and peace of Jesus Christ. Come up in your knowledge of unhealthy foods that may be having a devastating effect on your body, mind, and spirit. Come up in your understanding of your perceived need of certain harmful relationships. Come up in your attitude about yourself, and see the potential awaiting your grand entrance into the extraordinary as you seek the mind of Jesus Christ through much prayer and study of his ways of doing ordinary things daily. Come up and be different: be better informed, better educated, and better known for the best in you as you seek the best in others, thereby seeing a newer you mirrored in them.

The key to inner peace and safe arrival at one's destination is knowing the lay of the land in which you travel. A game hunter always studies the lay of the land before he ventures out to seek his prey. Knowing the lay of the land helps one avoid concealed pitfalls and crevices, both natural and man-made.

Knowing the lay of the land encourages one to venture further into the vast unknown, even if that unknown is within and personal. Being familiar with the hidden and not-so-obvious obstacles in life can prolong life and enhance healthy growth. Growth is no respecter of persons or gender but is a key to longevity and peace of mind. Seek to know the lay of the land, and always seek the high ground, thereby avoiding the unseen pitfalls of ignorance.

Know This

If any man will do His will, he shall know of the doctrine.

—John 7:17 (KJV)

If we are to grow spiritually, we must will to be obedient to the Spirit of God. If persons desire scientific knowledge, their intellectual curiosity will lead them to intellectual studies. If they desire spiritual knowledge, learning what Jesus teaches, they must be obedient to the small things they already know about God first.

Spiritual darkness is always the result of disobedience. Intellectual darkness stems from ignorance. Spiritual darkness comes from disobedience; there is perversity somewhere within that you absolutely refuse to turn loose. We ask, "Why do I not understand this? Everyone seems to understand the Bible lessons except me! The seemingly simple sermons just go over my head. Why do I feel so left out?"

No one ever receives a word from God without being immediately tested. The Word of God hits us right where we are. His Word searches out the smallest nooks and crannies and identifies or reminds us of their presence so that we may confess them with the mouth in repentance. Do not shirk what God has discovered in you because if you do, you will suffer the more for your disobedience and may continue even deeper into spiritual darkness.

Never revive memories of stolen kisses in the past lest the realities of the present suffer loss and misery becomes your constant companion.

Let Him Witness to You

The Spirit himself testifies with our spirit
that we are God's children.

—Romans 8:16

We are in danger of developing a barter spirit when we
come to the Lord. To barter means to trade or exchange
one thing for another. When we come to the Lord, most
of us at one time or another, maybe during some trials or
troubles, want to see a sign before we obey what he has
shown us. You ask: "Why has not God revealed himself to
me, shown me a sign, done something unusual?"

Well, he cannot. Not that he will not; but he cannot if
you're stuck in the middle of the road and absolutely will
not abandon yourself to his will. As soon as you do, God
will witness to himself. He cannot witness to you, but he
will immediately witness to his own nature in you. If you
had experienced the witness before, the reality in your
journey could end up being a sentimental journey, and the
slightest bump in the road would have derailed your walk.
But once you move in the redemptive Spirit and stop that
godless debate over what God wants you to do, God will
give you the witness.

As soon as you stop that reasoning argument, God
witnesses to what he has done, and you will see the silliness
of the argument you had beforehand. Never debate before

God! If you are debating whether God can deliver from sin, either let him do it or tell him he cannot. "Come to me, all ye who are weary and burdened, and I will give you rest." The Spirit of God witnesses to the redemption of our Lord, and he does not witness to anything else.

The simplicity of our natural common-sense reasoning may easily be mistaken for the witness of the Holy Spirit, but the Spirit witnesses to his own nature and the work of redemption, never to our reasoning.

> And let us return to the LORD; for He has
> torn, but He will heal us.
>
> —Hosea 6:1 (NKJV)

When followers of Christ are under the stress of going through a test of their faith, we are apt to lose touch with and forget the mystical, supernatural touch of God. We become focused on the pains associated with what we're facing and vindicating ourselves as the cause of our own suffering until we no longer look to God as anything other than as a subject of sentimental discussion.

If you have been obliterating the serious presence of God in your life, stop and review your circumstances, and see when and where God has not been first and foremost. Have you substituted your ideas of holiness, service, or your temperamental abilities—your organizational or denominational creed or doctrine?

This has nothing to do with salvation; it is rather abandonment of yourself to Jesus Christ. From Jesus's point of view the only good thing in this is whether we are in union with himself. He is not concerned at all with why we have an attitude; he is only concerned that we adopt the correct attitude. To follow Christ is not a physical effort but a way of life anchored by the desire and dogged determination in our spirit to be one with him at all costs. Everything else is secondary. Let us return to him in our storm and see the salvation of the Lord up close and personal. When we do, we'll see that the storm is only a fading memory, soon to be replaced by unspeakable joy.

> Turn to me and be gracious to me,
> for I am lonely and afflicted.
> The troubles of my heart have multiplied;
> free me from my anguish.

> —Psalm 25:16–17 (NIV 1984)

When God separates you in your afflictions, whether it be sickness, divorce, alienation of affections from another, depression, or loneliness, he will do as he did in training the twelve. He will move you away from those things that so easily beset you and expound on some things to you more clearly.

When we are engrossed in our perceived need for human companionship (male or female), our human nature commands our full attention and immediate gratification. But Jesus, knowing this, orchestrates our situation so he can have us alone to himself, where he can expound some things to us more clearly. If we are truly his, the only thing that should be clear to us is the way he deals with our souls. We speak with our brothers about their afflictions and, we sympathize, but until God gives us a similar affliction, we cannot fully understand our brothers' pains.

God doesn't deliver us *from* afflictions but delivers us *in* our afflictions. Afflictions may endure for a season, but every season has an end. Every affliction is either internal or external in origin. Either way it is orchestrated by God for His glory.

> For Christ did not send me to baptize, but to preach the gospel—not with words of human wisdom, lest the cross of Christ be emptied of its power.
>
> —1 Corinthians 1:17 (NIV 1984)

In today's piety movement it is chic to say when on the mountaintop, "Lord, send me." In the mind of many there is sentimental value in being able to say to those around us, "I went to darkest Africa," or "The Lord found favor with me, so I'm going to …"

Paul did not go on his missionary journeys in a quest for egocentric applause but only obeyed the vision given him on the road to Damascus. He had no concern about the currency of his day or anything else that would cause him to be focused on anything but the cause of Jesus Christ. And he'd been told how much he would suffer for the Name.

Now that I'm on this missionary journey, I realize he didn't send me to become puffed up about matters bound up in the providence of God, lest the cross of Jesus be brought to no effect. When there is no applause but only tough times, my crying, complaining, and agonizing over situations which God orchestrated for His glory and my edification do not glorify the living God in the highest but further reinforce Matthew 22:14: "For many be called, but few chosen."

He sent me not to *do* anything but to *be* all things in Christ. I must accept the lack, the dross, the loneliness and must also refute the gossip which makes me think I am wonderfully worthy of my calling.

"If anyone serves, he should do it with the strength God provides, so that in all things God may be praised" (1 Peter 4:11 NIV 1984).

> Now stay here tonight as the others did, and
> I will find out what else the Lord will tell me.
>
> —Numbers 22:19 (NIV 1984)

Only the most devoted and sincere followers of Christ will arrive at the conclusion that God orchestrates circumstances. The sovereign God of all creation frequently does not move or speak in ways we typically understand and comprehend. His communications to us, his creation, however, will always be in a realm that is possible for mortal humans to grasp, even though it may require extraordinary diligence.

Tonight is your night for many to hear from the Lord. Naturally, it is nighttime here as I communicate to you, the reader, what God desires you to know about your situation. For some he chooses the night of hardships in your life to speak to your situation. For others, quiet evenings are the only time you will allow yourself to be still as you rest and recuperate for the coming dawn. For you, this is his time to communicate his will for you and, in many instances, respond to your plea for deliverance.

For some, the circumstances surrounding your immediate situation were and are orchestrated by God even though your understanding may not be what you desire. God will never allow more to come upon you than you can bear. Many will understand this and be obedient to the Word of God, and their deliverance will blaze forth with the coming dawn.

When God gives a saint a vision and that saint does not immediately respond, he will always come down with a different point of view. Be obedient to the vision, and reap the best God has to offer his disciples in Christ Jesus.

Lovers' dreams

A lover's glee is kisses sweet
And hugs throughout the night.
And every day a holiday,
A dreamer's way of life.

Reality is a different thing;

There's always bills to pay
And food that's always in demand.
This stuff won't go away.

But lovers dream of kisses sweet.
For some, for real it's true;
For others, just a fading hope,
Just something else to do.

But love is not a tangible thing,
Not something on a rack,
Or something on a dollar bill.
It's action that we lack.

Feed My Sheep Not a Creed

Lovest thou me? … Feed my sheep.

—John 21:17 (KJV)

"Don't think about it, dwell on it, discuss it with someone else, but feed my sheep! See to it that they are nourished, groomed, protected, and taught whatever I have taught you.

"Show them whatever I have shown you. Don't teach them a creed, your way of thinking, or your way of accomplishing a task I have given you."

Jesus Christ did whatever his Father directed to him to do. He said what his Father directed him to say, when he told him to say it. Very specific! We sometimes count as service what we do in the name of and for a creed. Our discipleship is based on devotion to Jesus Christ, not to adherence to a creed. There are no ifs, ands, buts, or conditions, just simply: "If any man come to me and hate not [all else], he cannot be my disciple" (Luke 14:26 KJV).

"If you are my disciple, you must be devoted to me!" People don't want to be devoted to Jesus, only to the cause he started. Devotion to Jesus Christ is a deeply rooted offense to the educated mind of today, which refuses to accept him in any capacity other than a philosophical comrade. The abandoned saint is devoted wholly to Jesus Christ, and the Spirit of Christ residing in him will testify of his presence.

Momentary Doubt

Are you the one who was to come, or should we expect someone else?

—Matthew 11:3 (NIV 1984)

The danger of momentary doubt is that it automatically challenges our stability in a right-now, ever-present God. Immediately spiritual leakage begins, and we begin a downward spiral to a different point of view. Spiritual leakage, whether yesterday, now, or in the future, must be identified, acknowledged, cauterized, and immediately disposed of. Hebrews 4:12: "Sharper than any two-edged sword" is God's Word.

Move Immediately

Move quickly, because that will mean the
LORD has gone out in front.

—2 Samuel 5:24

When God enters the annals of your mind and compels you
to do a thing, the urgency that accompanies that thing will
not rest because the Spirit of God has detected an element
in your character that corresponds to his character. Do not
hesitate, estimate, or approximate. If you do, you will lose
the divine urgency the Holy Spirit has placed in your spirit.

Move Quickly!

Let the peace of Christ rule in your hearts.

—Colossians 3:15

There are times when things in your life in Christ will seem
to fall apart and the spirit of peace will not witness. When
this happens, and at some point it will, run immediately
to him and ask why. But do so quickly before you come
down with a different point of view. Never allow anything
to fester that separates you from the face of Jesus Christ.
When the matter is identified and corrected, the spirit of
peace will witness, and right away things become crystal
clear.

When you find all the bits and pieces that caused the wreck in your life, take them as things to wrestle against and not suffer. If this thing is not identified and dealt with, you will assume a spirit of self-pity. Never put on a cloak of self-righteousness and say, "This is caused by the devil or my enemy or my friend, not by me."

The life in Christ should be like that of a child. Ask Christ to give you his consciousness, and when he does, the Spirit of peace will witness. In his consciousness we are not self-conscious. The child is not conscious of the will of God; he instantly obeys without consciousness.

God says, "Through opposition you have grown much, and your abilities now surpass that which you used to have. True, you haven't moved a rock. But your calling was to be obedient and to push and to exercise your faith and trust in my wisdom. That you have done. Now I, my friend, will move the rock."

At times, when we hear a word from God, we tend to use our own intellect to decipher his motives and thoughts; when what God wants is just simple obedience and faith in him. Exercise the faith that moves mountains, but know that it is still God who moves the mountains.

When everything seems to go wrong … just P.U.S.H.

When the job gets you down … just P.U.S.H.

When people don't do as you think they should … just P.U.S.H.

When your money is gone and the bills are due … just P.U.S.H.

When people just don't understand you … just P.U.S.H.

P = Pray

U = Until

S = Something

H = Happens

I will show him how much he must suffer for my name.

—Acts 9:16

The common view among the masses is that the ministry of the Christian church is building things to help Christ in his ministry: television, billion-dollar advertising budgets, and glamorized personalities advertising church services. But if one is truly going to be used of God, look to be taken through a multitude of experiences that are not experiences you would typically welcome. They are meant to make you useful in the Master's hands. When Jesus died on the cross, his agony was not for ordinary men. He suffered "according to the will of God," not from a personal point of view.

One purpose of your experiences is to acquaint you with what transpires in the life of others, so you won't be surprised when you encounter this or that in other souls. "I hate this one," "She just talks too much," "They lied to me," "They said this or that," "They were rude!"

It is only when we are rightly related to Jesus Christ that we can understand what God is trying to accomplish when he deals with us. We're not used to literally suffering physically, emotionally, or spiritually. We're used to taking shortcuts to win the favor of God in our lives. Are we partakers in Christ's suffering? Are we prepared to let go of our egos, reputations, and ambitions, to allow God to destroy our individual determination? We seldom realize what God is after in dealing with us, so we follow along out of legalism or force of habit instead of following in blind faith and love.

> For we are God's fellow workers; you are
> God's field, God's building.
>
> —1 Corinthians 3:9 (NASB)

Be very careful you do not get into a situation of labor that keeps you from concentrating on Jesus Christ. Many, many Christians worship their work and the affirmation their work affords. The primary concern of the Christian worker should be concentrating on God as his focus and remaining focused on the tasks at hand. God will assure that the focus of the worker is not compromised by the demands of the job when the Spirit of God attends.

When a Christian's focus is on his work to the exclusion of the presence of the Holy Spirit, his or her work is apt to become their central theme in life, and gradually the joy they first experienced when they were introduced to God will dissipate. At that point any task associated with the ministry of Jesus Christ becomes burdensome and a thing to avoid; from there, other things grievous to the Holy Spirit evolve.

There is nothing in life so hurtful that the favor of God cannot heal it. But the presence of God will only be manifested where there is a welcome mat at the heart's door. We have no moral right to judge when and where we receive Him or under what circumstances, because He engineers the circumstances that surround us.

Never allow your devotion to your job to rob you of the best God has to offer. You must not sell your birthright for a pot of stew, because you will never get past the consequences.

> Whoever does not love does not know God,
> because God is love.
>
> —1 John 4:8

These are the times that try men's souls, and many are running to and fro seeking answers to their many complex problems. Many of our human problems are personal in that we caused them by something we either did or neglected to do in our lives. We tend to devote much time and effort to those things we love, and the things we love most are designated priority number one in a descending order from the most important to the least important. And we live our lives in accordance with the priorities we place on day-to-day issues.

One of the top priorities in many of our lives is what we commonly refer to as love, which ordinarily in practice can be expressed as *phyllo*: love of flesh, sex masquerading as *agape*: a higher godly form of true love (both Greek terms). But for Christians or disciples of Jesus Christ, the *agape* love of God will lead them to seek a solution or solutions from the One with whom they are in love, for God is love in its highest form of expression.

This love between the created (human) and the creator (God) is manifested in a covenant between humankind and God which guarantees the protection, welfare, and complete oversight of every woman, man, and child. Why worry and fret over things you cannot control? All that that is required of us, his creation, is to believe his promises, acknowledge him, seek his forgiveness, and learn to love him as he loves us. The process is initiated by prayer.

Ask and you will receive, and your joy will be
complete. (John 16:24)

Even in laughter the heart may ache, and joy
may end in grief. (Proverbs 14:13)

My natural mind recalls with delight the days of laughter
and happy events I thought would never end. So all I did
or dreamed of doing was aimed at recapturing those
moments in time when I knew no pain, and so life goes. I
was ever-expecting moments of gladness but then one day,
perhaps in a moment in time, in the twinkling of an eye,
calamity overtook me, and my mind was filled with dread,
not only of the moment but even of tomorrow, though
tomorrow hadn't yet arrived!

My lesson in this episode of living reminded me of just how
fragile life and all its components can be. But my Bible tells
me "weeping endures for a night but joy cometh in the
morning." Then I discovered by the length of my suffering
that night and day are not necessarily related to each other
but are only segments that separate my despair.

They separate it according to the severity of the suffering,
and that is determined by almighty God. But he has already
assured me: "I will never leave you nor forsake you." So why
am I suffering at all? In my suffering I am made strong,
and I am thankful for being selected to suffer as an under-
shepherd in Christ.

My Lord Indeed

Ye call me Master and Lord: and ye say well;
for so I am.

—John 13:13 (KJV)

One of the obstacles facing saints is the belief that we must
be obedient to someone whether we see them as equals or
greater than we. And that is where many of us walk with
him no more. But Jesus never insisted on having authority
over anyone and never said: "Thou shalt" or "Thou wilt do
this or that." He leaves us free to do whatever we desire to
the extent that we can insult him, curse him, and berate
him to the lowest level of which we're capable.

And he never says a word. But when his life has been
created in me by his redemption, then I recognize that
he has absolute authority over me. He owns me by his
redemptive blood. Then I instantly realize he has complete
authority over me, and for me to refuse to acknowledge
this is an insult to the Holy Spirit.

I am not my own but have been bought and paid for by
the blood of Jesus. I am not my own and have no right
to myself. Although he has given me the opportunity to
pick and choose whom I will serve, it is far better for me
eternally to choose him. The revelation of my growth in
grace is the way in which I see my obedience to him. Am
I obedient to his will or my own?

My Part

The woman whom thou gavest to be with
me, she gave me …

—Genesis 3:12 (KJV)

The term *me* is used to identify oneself specifically as the
object of attention. Of course, it was used repeatedly by
our Lord and Savior Jesus Christ to identify himself as the
one and only God, willing and able to perform a task at
that moment in time. Jesus said, "Whoever enters through
me shall be saved." "I am the one and only God (there are
many false gods) who can save humanity from eternal
damnation."

Adam was specific but truthful to his eternal peril when
he stated, "She gave *me*, and I did eat." His wife, Eve,
likewise did admit her conspiracy with Satan: "The serpent
deceived *me*, and I did eat."

The term *me* excludes all others as a part of an action,
attitude, or philosophy. It says, "I and I alone am responsible
for whatever consequences result from whatever I have
done, said, or thought. The responsibility for the sins in
my life rests on me alone, not wholly because of my genetic
connection with the original sinful parents, but because of
my current entrapment by the lures of the flesh."

It can be said then that I am extremely caught in a web not of my making. But an opposing and equally strong extreme says, "Yes, but the other 'me' says I and I alone am able to rescue and save you from your genetic death sentence by the deliverer '*me*' in Jesus Christ."

Choose you this day which me you will follow: the *me* in you or the *me* in Jesus Christ. Eventually a choice must be made, deliberately or by default. Choose the *me* in God and live, or the *me* in your flesh by default and die.

My Part

God has shown me how to love Him;
His grace will ever be
A driving force in goodness, for all eternity.
His love is shown in many ways in manifested truths. And as we learn the will of God,

Our faith will be renewed.
And as we grow in wisdom still, we just begin to see The goodness of this holy wine
Was pressed for you and me.
Each one of us must play a part in God's divine Delight, to help fulfill

What Adam failed in Satan's dirty fight.
No, don't give up as Adam did, and hide behind a leaf, 'Cause God has shown us what to do.
It's all in our belief.

Now this is just a poem to some, but some will see a truth,
But let us all think godliness
And give our God his due.
My Prayer in Praise

4:15 a.m., June 21, 2011

Though I walk among men of stature whose understanding and wisdom equal none, there is one who is above all, known by few and subject to no one, whose deeds are many and countless in understanding. He is revered by few and needed by all. I am created by him who moves on the surfaces of the wind, during the fire, and exists in the depths of the seas. I am made after him, and my will is subject to the will of Jesus, for we are one in spirit.

Today, while it is still today, I pray for all who are given to me to pray for. In this early hour the Spirit of God walks among the likes of himself, seeking those who will do his will among men and during times such as this.

"Oh mighty, wonderful, wise aged of ages, Father of all, mother to the motherless and doctor to the ailing. I will tell the world of thy goodness and truth during the fire. You ride the crests of the winds and stay the flight of the flying terror in my midst. Thou art God, and above thee there is no other.

"Speak to thy servant this morning for thou art in the volume of the books. I am here and you are here with me, and I crave to hear thy words this morning in the depth of my heart, mind, body, and spirit. Speak thou, O King of kings, for thy servant is listening."

> But do not use your freedom to indulge the
> sinful nature.

—Galatians 5:13

I am made free to walk in the newness of life in Jesus Christ rather than to manifest carnality through the preaching of hatred, racial bias, or anything that opposes the divine will of our eternal God.

A born again, spiritually minded individual will never suggest or say to you, "Believe this and that," but will suggest that you manifest in your life the standards of Jesus Christ. I am free to exhibit the love of God by guarding my tongue from speaking vague innuendoes against anyone, whether it is in support of my national interests or in defense of Jesus Christ and his righteousness.

Always keep your life measured by the standards of Jesus. The name *Christian* by biblical definition speaks of those who have decided to follow and adhere to the teachings of Jesus Christ (Acts 11:26). While many have sought to make its proper use the name of a denomination, its original meaning is a noble one, of which any follower of Christ can rightly be proud.

There is only one liberty, the liberty of Jesus at work in our conscience enabling us to do what is right in Jesus Christ. Pray for those whom you perceive to be "not like you," whether they be black, white, orange or green. We all have the same heavenly Father, and all blood is red and runs freely from lacerations, whatever the color of the skin. Be patient as God is patient with you.

> All things work together for good to them
> that love God.
>
> —Romans 8:28 (KJV)

When I accepted God into my life, I entered into a relationship like no other except that of a parent and child. In my life, everything is in the hand of God, and it is he who orchestrates the circumstances in which I find myself.

God brings things into my life that I cannot at all understand. But the Holy Spirit understands. God is bringing me into places and circumstances and among people who are right in the palm of God's hand. I can never put my hand in front of my face and say, "This is best for me, and I'll do this and not that." This is an insult to the Lord, for I am saying to him, "You're not able to guide me to where I need to be. I know better than you what's best for me, for I determine my future and my destination." That is scripturally unsound.

My part in intercessory prayer is not to enter the agony of intercession, but to utilize the common-sense circumstances in which God has placed me and the common-sense people he puts me among by his providence. Am I making the work of the Holy Spirit difficult by being indefinite or by trying to do his work for him? I will do the human side of intercession, and the human side involves the circumstances I am in and the people to whom I am connected.

> My son, do not despise the chastening of
> the Lord, Nor be discouraged when you are
> rebuked by Him.
>
> —Hebrews 12:5 (NKJV)

It is very easy to become disheartened and quench the Spirit of God when we do not immediately understand what he is after. We quench the Spirit by despising the chastening of the Lord and especially when it comes through another person, even though he or she be used of God for that purpose. If we have only a shallow experience of sanctification, we mistake the shadow for the reality or the "real thing" when God starts to check, and then we say, "Oh, this is the devil," or we claim someone has picked us out for personal attack.

Never quench the Spirit, and don't despise him when he says to you—"Don't continue being ignorant of my presence; you are not where you ought to be." Let him relate you rightly to God. Don't say, "Oh, I just can't help it. I prayed, and things still turned out that way, so I'm going to just quit."

Are you prepared to let God have his way with you on his terms, or do you want to set the standards of sanctification?

In the year that King Uzziah died I saw also
the Lord sitting upon a throne.

—Isaiah 6:1 (KJV)

My historical path is fraught with instances of God moving heroes in and out of my life. There are times I don't understand the will of God in these matters because his will for me is causing conflict with my need for Uzziah, whom he has moved or is in the process of moving from my life. But he has to move Uzziah out of my life, so he can bring more of himself into that position. And this is where the faint of heart and those who are determined to steer the course part company, "for many are invited, but few are chosen" (Matthew 22:14).

This is the time when Uzziah comforted, accommodated, compromised, and cried with me. My Uzziah did all for me that God stands for, but Uzziah is not the living God and, due to Uzziah's inherited weaknesses, can only offer spiritually crippling sympathy. My view of God is dependent upon my willingness to allow his Spirit to fill me with his knowledge of what is best for me to the glory of God. My path must be God first, God second, and God third until my focus is steadfast on the face of Jesus Christ and not on Uzziah. If you but steer the course and look steadfastly on the face of Jesus, Uzziah will become only a shadow, like a vapor passing before your eyes.

Never a Disputing Saint

I want men everywhere to lift up holy hands
in prayer, without anger or disputing.

—1 Timothy 2:8

The saint, by virtue of having been declared worthy of being called a saint, will not be found among those who dispute the oracles of holiness but will dwell with those who offer up praises to almighty God. Things that have been found to be true, praiseworthy, honorable, and peaceful that soothe a troubled mind are not worthy of dispute among the redeemed of God.

Prayer during a storm will often bring calm to a raging sea and boisterous winds. In every uncertainty regarding the will of almighty God in any circumstance, the potential for dispute arises, and Satan will soon make his presence known by the intensity of the disputation.

Never Alone in Trouble

Who comforts us in all our troubles, so
that we can comfort those in any trouble
with the comfort we ourselves have received
from God.

—2 Corinthians 1:4

Many followers of Christ believe that a life in Christ means
deliverance *from* all troubles, but it means deliverance *in*
troubles, which is far different.

"He that dwelleth in the secret place of the most High ...
There shall no evil befall thee" (Psalm 91:1, 10 KJV). No plague
will come near you when you are in Christ. Certainly there
will be many troubles, but God doesn't deliver you from
them—that is, take you out of the path of troubles—but
delivers you and me during our troubles. Jesus, because of
who he was, expected troubles, just as all who follow Christ
then and now can expect troubles. Nevertheless, Jesus said,
"But take heart! I have overcome the world" (John 16:33).

Certainly, tribulation will come, but for those in Christ
Jesus there is no need to fear because we are all in the
hands of God: "In the world ye shall have tribulation: but
be of good cheer; I have overcome the world." God does not
give us overcoming life but life as we overcome. So don't be
overly concerned about tomorrow; the overcoming power

today prepares us for the challenges we face tomorrow if we're still here.

Overcome your own timidity about relying on God's grace to see you through today. Overcome your timidity in accepting the truths of God's will for you in Christ Jesus. When we accept and embrace the fullness of Jesus Christ in our lives, overcoming power is present.

Nevertheless

Nevertheless ...

—Job 17:9

The tendency to veer from truth (Jeremiah 2:36) to the realms of darkness is imbedded in my fallen nature. However, there is a guarantee of my survival anchored in the promises of him who is the creator and guarantor of godly promises to those who will hold their ways steadfast in every holy pursuit.

Every aspect of my living needs to manifest cleanliness, from the top of my head to the soles of my feet, from the rising of the sun in the morning until the going down of the same, and from my first conscious thoughts until I close my eyes in death. Let my hands forever be clean through washing in Christ's righteousness. Amen.

New Day on the Horizon

For as he thinketh in his heart, so is he: Eat
and drink, saith he to thee, but his heart is
not with thee.

—Proverbs 23:7

For the disciples of Jesus Christ and others who follow
his teachings as contained in Holy Scripture, it comes as
no surprise that the prophecies of the apostolic fathers
are being revealed daily to the disbelief and horror of
millions, who base their hope of physical survival on the
wisdom of humans sitting in places of authority ordained
by other humans.

Many have been and are being duped by those who are
blinded by their own form of morality; every person
lives by their own value system and teaches it to those
around them. In their dream world no one is intimidated
or insulted, and everyone lives in peace and harmony.
Everything, every lifestyle, every agenda, and all things
financial are not only tolerated but encouraged. Let no
one be offended or angered, for they are their own God.

We cannot accept the theory that in every man, woman,
and child there exists a spiritual component that is ever
working to determine one's fate in this life and the life to
come. During eras such as these, times are changing, and
one would do well to consider the words referenced in the

above scriptures and others referring to this dispensation. For every action, attitude, agenda, thesis, dogma, or creed, there is and will be a consequence. Everything under the sun will be judged by the Holy One.

No God, no Peace

Peace I leave with you; my peace I give you…
Do not let your hearts be troubled.

—John 14:27

If a personal endeavor becomes burdensome and appears out of my control, I am apt to blame God, but I am the one at fault, because there is something—some sort of perversity somewhere—that I will not release. As long as I try to serve two gods, the Spirit of peace will not witness. When I, by my will, determine to rely completely on the living God, things will become clear.

If, in the beginning, I started this endeavor in the will of God but turn my focus from him to another god, I immediately lose my guidance, and confusion reigns in my mortal body. When the Spirit of peace is absent, seek him, and you'll find if you are honest and focused on God instead of another that any problem which separates you from God is born of disobedience, and disaster will follow. The key to spiritual peace is obedience. Many problems will arrive, but God knows and will take care of me. I must be obedient.

> Afterward Jesus appeared in a different
> form to two of them while they were walking
> in the country.

—Mark 16:12

The way of the ordinary is exceedingly hard, for there is always in the heart of every human the inbred invitation to come up. But for those who have elected to come up and made their calling and election sure, there exist two challenges. The first is to remain in the carnal ordinary state. The second is to escape the ordinary and ascend to the extraordinary. Both states present their own challenges. It is by divine will that the saint battles in the hedges and byways of ordinary, everyday living which presents its own uniqueness. To come up, saints must climb beyond the ordinary, which demands constant devotion to their climb while resisting the invitation of the devil to remain ordinary. Will you come up and leave all that you love behind or will you elect to remain ordinary? Either choice comes with a god of your choosing.

No Need to Shout

> But even so, the quiet words of a wise man
> are better than the shout of a king of fools.

—Ecclesiastes 9:17 (TLB)

The carnal mind is not concerned with the truth, life, or sustaining aspects of divine wisdom. Neither can it be, for the carnal mind is conditioned by life's experiences, which are devoid of godly guidance and direction. In the midst of such an environment, loud speaking or shouting to gain attention is expected and affirmed in some quarters and in many instances. Anything less is considered not worthy of consideration for positions of authority.

Beware of a spirit of anxiety, which leads to speaking before hearing the whole of a matter. Followers of Christ should avoid being anxious, for this will ultimately lead to vain or untimely words spoken in haste. "Everyone should be quick to listen, slow to speak and slow to become angry" (James 1:19).

> Now is the time of their confusion.
>
> —Micah 7:4

Whenever a thing is before you and the Spirit of peace does not witness, there will be confusion, and invariably, confusion is the result of disobedience in some area of your life. The confusion may be the result of disobedience in an earlier matter where confusion was present, and the matter never resolved to the satisfaction of almighty God. Disobedience has no place in the life of a saint, and when a matter is not brought before God in prayer for resolution, it will linger in one form or another until resolved to the satisfaction of almighty God. If there is confusion in your life, don't sleep on it or talk it over with a favored aunt or uncle, but immediately search out the area of disobedience, and once it is identified, be obedient to the smallest detail. Never try to reason it out, justify something, or say "If only this or that thing had not occurred ..." But it did occur, whatever the matter is!

No Vision, Now What?

You ought to live holy and godly lives.

—2 Peter 3:11

There are times when my vision will no longer be there: no congregation, no bystanders, etc. That's when I need the almighty grace of God to take me to the next step in devotion in my study, in my reading, even in my preferred place of study: my office, my garage, etc. No enthusiasm, no anything! It takes a lot more grace then because I can easily slip into laziness. It takes a dogged, conscious determination to draw on the grace of God and do that. Every Christian must partake in the reality of the incarnation—to bring that thing down into the reality of flesh and blood—and that requires a dogged determination by force of will.

We become disquieted in our spirits when there is no vision, and soon our minds acquire a sentimental memory of past visions when the thought of Jesus was just a dream consisting of good feelings. Ask God to give you back your vision. "Create in me a clean heart and right attitude," "lest I fall into the snare of the devil."

> You did not choose me, but I chose you and
> appointed you to go and bear fruit—fruit

that will last. Then the Father will give you
whatever you ask in my name.

—John 15:16

We are not saved only to be a path for the Holy Ghost, but
to be sons and daughters of God. He did not turn us into
human switches for the sake of reaching the lost but into
spiritual messengers, and the message must be a part of
who we are. We *are* the message we carry to others.

Jesus was his own message; his words were spirit and life.
As his disciples, our lives must be the sacrament of our
message. We must be what we preach. Naturally, we will do
anything necessary to accomplish our spiritual agenda, but
it takes a heart broken by conviction of sin, baptized by the
Holy Ghost, and crumpled into the will of God for our lives
to be sacraments of our message. The difference between
preaching and giving a testimony is that the preacher has
realized the call of God and is determined to use all his
energy to proclaim the Word of God.

God destroys every egocentric idea we have about our
own lives and batters us into his own use. Before God's
message can liberate others, the liberation must be real in
us. Pentecost did not teach the disciples anything; it made
them the incarnation of what they preached—"Ye shall be
witnesses unto me."

Nothing to Fear but Fear

But the LORD your God himself will cross
over ahead of you.

—Deuteronomy 31:3 (NLT)

One must be afraid to be afraid to be victorious in the
army of the Lord. Most seasoned combat soldiers will
readily admit that when they are fearful of being afraid,
the battle in their mind is over. A soldier cannot be a
reliable opponent in the face of the enemy until the spirit
of fear is mastered.

When our God crosses over to assure victory, his splendor
and completion are manifested in many ways. His crossing
over is as a leader among and above all leaders known to
or by men; his crossing over says to his soldiers: "Follow me
and see the salvation of the Lord!" His crossing over says to
the weak and faint of heart: "You have nothing to fear, for I
have already overcome the enemy, but you must overcome
the enemy within you. Don't wait until tomorrow to cross
over after me, for you must work today while it is still today.

"If you hesitate and wrestle with the vision, I am showing
you, you will come down with a different point of view and
not cross over after me. I am Alpha and Omega, the first
and last, and beside me there is none other who can save
from the gutter-most to the uttermost. Follow me!"

If you were blind, you would not be guilty of
sin; but now that you claim you can see, your
guilt remains.

—John 9:41

During these days of instant gratification and cookie-
cutter religion it is common to hear someone claim to
be spiritually enlightened. Even during Bible class some
will quickly claim to *already know* the will of God in their
lives, so they have no need for further teaching! Can I in
all honesty say, "I can see clearly now, the rain is gone. I
can see all obstacles in my way"? Beware what you confess
with your mouth. The Lord does not suffer fools lightly,
the Bible declares. The inference is that only a fool would
so quickly make certain claims if not abandoned to Jesus
Christ and his righteousness.

Guard the heart for the Word of God tells us out of the
abundance of the heart the mouth speaks. It's not the
mouth that betrays a person but the content of the heart.
The mouth only speaks what the heart reveals. Whether
one is truly abandoned to Jesus Christ or not, the heart will
ultimately reveal. For if I claim to know God, and my heart
betrays my confession through the mouth, my sin remains,
and I'm guilty of grieving the Holy Spirit.

I will follow you, Lord; but ...

—Luke 9:61

For some of us the Spirit of God will say do this or do that; and when we give what he asks some thought, it dawns on us that this thing goes against our common sense. What do we do then? At the very least, we hesitate. What you do physically is what you do every time, all the time until you by sheer determination change that pattern. The same thing is true spiritually. You are confronted again and again by what God wants from you and in you, and you turn your back on him every time. And you will do that until you doggedly determine to be obedient to his will for you.

By habit, inclination, and orientation, we always choose our common-sense method of doing things physically and spiritually. God wants the same reckless abandonment to him that we manifest physically. Those who follow Christ will often be challenged to jump into some things in this life by faith—reckless abandonment to Jesus Christ. When we risk all, we know by common sense for all that Christ is spiritually, and we do so immediately, we find that he relieves all the doubts as we forsake our common-sense approach. He fills our situations by his presence. Trust God implicitly and when he brings you to a place of immediate decision, choose his way, and everything will become crystal clear.

> The dead were judged according to what they had done.

> —Revelation 20:12

The scriptures tell us that everyone must stand before the judgment seat of Christ. If we learn to live in the light of Jesus Christ as he is the light in this present time, judgment will encourage us to delight even more in working for our Lord.

Be ever focused on the judgment seat of Christ as you walk in the holiest of holies within you. A wrong attitude over what you see in another, a pious attitude, or a self-righteous, self-exalted view of your religion will land you on the side of Satan, and your view of Jesus Christ will only be a sentimental expression of shallowness. If the Spirit of God detects one or all of these, quickly take it before the Lord in prayer. "A little leaven leaveneth the whole lump." Pray, "Create in me a clean heart, O God, and renew a steadfast, humble spirit within me."

The penalty of sin is confirmation in sin. It's not only God who punishes us for sin, but sin confirms itself in the sinner, and consequences follow. No amount of struggling and praying will stop you from doing some things; if you continue doing them you become used to them and no longer see them as sin. Instead of judging, walk in the same light you want to see in another; intercede for them before God.

> When they saw the courage of Peter and John and realized that they were unschooled, ordinary men, they were astonished and they took note that these men had been with Jesus.

—Acts 4:13

Courage, perseverance, and the will to see beyond Jordan is the beginning of a spiritual foundation from which a saint must ascend to gain extraordinary faith in God. There is nothing spectacular about being ordinary unless ordinary saints are striving to master the utmost in themselves toward their highest potential in Jesus Christ.

A saint must prove faithful in ordinary things in Christ. This precedes extraordinary trials, which result in extraordinary blessings and favor of God. Ordinary turmoil of everyday living will either harden saints' dogged determination to remain true to their vision of Jesus or will cause them to lose their vision of Jesus through the frustration of waiting to see Jesus as he is. Their view of Jesus was too small. Extraordinary saints will never wait for a manifestation of Jesus because they have already seen him as he is, and no further proof is required.

> When they saw the courage of Peter and John and realized that they were unschooled, ordinary men, they were astonished and they took note that these men had been with Jesus.

—Acts 4:13

Many consider that there is a need in this life for more and better education: elementary, high school, college, and in some cases graduate studies are required so that the student receives recognition and accreditation for certain types of employment. However, Peter and John were not seminary educated and not trained in psychology or basic elementary education. Neither had they been awarded a degree in biblical literacy. But they were filled with the Spirit of God, endowed with extraordinary gifts and were prepared to do extraordinary things that glorified God.

Are you an ordinary saint doing extraordinary work for the Lord or an ordinary church member waiting for some sort of celestial invitation to come up higher? The saint who is abandoned to Jesus Christ is an ordinary church member who has already received the vision to *come up higher* and is doing extraordinary things in the ministry of Jesus Christ.

> When they saw the courage of Peter and John and realized that they were unschooled, ordinary men, they were astonished and they took note that these men had been with Jesus.
>
> —Acts 4:13

Never dwell on and become mentally fixed on your inabilities and fears, because they are mere preparation for doing extraordinary things in the power of God. Every victory won by saints of God begins in ordinary ways doing ordinary things. The victorious-minded saints see and live in the realm of the ordinary, for their ordinary view of Jesus takes them far beyond the brink of ordinary accomplishments and into the realm of the ordinarily impossible. But all things are possible for those who believe he can.

With God all things are possible.

(Matthew 19:26)

The will is strengthened by a dogged determination to rise above the ordinary and ascend to heights far beyond what is ordinary in everyday living. "I can't do this; I can't see this; I can't feel this or that," are all predicated on being fixed in an ordinary self-defeating frame of mind which has all but removed the will of God from the equation.

Saints whose minds are fixed on escaping from life's challenges will never rise above the ordinary, for their view of God is limited to their natural fears and limitations. Never run from the challenge God has placed before you, because you are where you are by his divine will.

Quench not the light.

—2 Samuel 21:17 (KJV)

Beware of losing your focus on God while during your Red Sea experience. There are times when God must bring us to a place of pain and suffering before we see what he's after. Our natural reaction is to seek the reason for our suffering in places of familiarity, things with which we are familiar, people who have shown an obvious dislike for us. Many times, the people we dislike most or those who have shown a dislike for us are the ones God uses as instruments in our barrel of affliction.

During your Red Sea experience the voice of God speaks as a spirit of peace and steadfastness of mind. But we are too occupied with past disappointments and distrust of others, and we seek solace in loud, boisterous places of familiarity. "The Lord was not in the wind, the fire, or the earthquake" (1 Kings 19:11–12). Suppose God has brought you into a crisis and you don't go all the way but stop because you were distracted by something of more value to you than obedience to God.

He will engineer that crisis again but not as keen as before. You'll have to listen more intently this time to hear the voice of God while being more aware of your circumstances this time than ever before. There will be more humiliation this time around, and the view that held you spellbound before might prove to be like fool's gold with only a fading memory of what once seemed the pinnacle of answered prayers. But if you go through the crisis humbly, there will be praises to God as never before. Be very careful you don't shun the light of God in your life.

But we see Jesus.

—Hebrews 2:9

Have you ever been in despair and prayed and prayed for God to intervene in your situation, and it seemed your prayers were not going beyond the ceiling? There are times when Jesus cannot reveal himself in his royal apparel accompanied by a host of angels. But he comes to you in the middle of your dilemma as a poor beggar, seeking your immediate attention. You must turn from your problems, and while your attention is on another and not yourself, you grow in spiritual strength.

And there are times when he cannot reveal himself in any other way than in his majestic glory, so you may be uplifted and your prayers affirmed because you steadfastly focused on him. "Those who seek me, find me." When you see him, be prepared to acknowledge him in whatever form he appears because it is always good, and deliverance is at hand, but your focus must be on him and not what you perceive as the cause of your dilemma. He already knows all about it, but your humble submission is what he is after.

Acknowledge him ... He will appear.

—Hosea 6:3

Remember those earlier days.

—Hebrews 10:32

I learned early in life to mentally categorize everything and do all things according to a mental priority assigned to that task. I have learned through circumstances and the Word of God that consequences accompany every act, deliberate or otherwise.

Some things I chose to remember and some, to forget. I find it easy to remember the many blessings bestowed on me and mine, often coming quite unexpectedly and at odd times, but always received with glee and thanksgiving. The days on the mount always refresh present moments and give hope during times of stress. Then there are times I'd much rather forget. Whether there were circumstances that had to be dealt with or immediate difficulties brought on by unwise decisions, it becomes a matter of what I choose to remember. I had and still have that choice. Past and present circumstances and consequences must be dealt with and not denied in cases of pain or other unpleasantness.

But I've found that a determined spirit bolstered by a made-up mind gets me "over the hump" every time! I literally take God at his Word: "My grace is sufficient" (2 Corinthians 12:9). Despite my sinful nature, with all my "baggage," I have found favor with him (1 Timothy 1:12). Why would I not serve a God like that?

Saints of God, be encouraged. The best is yet to come.

> Restore to me the joy of your salvation and
> grant me a willing spirit …
>
> Then I will teach transgressors your ways,
> and sinners will turn back to you.
>
> —Psalm 51:12–13

We are never going through a trial just for our own spiritual enlightenment but also for the sake of others, that we may share with them the joy of overcoming the trials and tribulations common to people of God. As we overcome, we are being prepared to demonstrate overcoming, as lights overcome the darkness. As physical beings, we are most clearly taught by what is seen and heard with our natural physical abilities. God often uses the physical to demonstrate the spiritual.

When we are seen to physically endure hardship with a determination to endure whatever God allows to come our way, we strengthen and encourage others not only by our preaching but by demonstrating what we say, "*as an example of patience in the face of suffering.*" Then many will turn back from thinking defeat to believing that all things are possible with God. Never entertain the thought that you are being put upon by God for the sake of showing you off in his heavenly showcase as you go through your Red Sea experiences. You must be strengthened and delivered in your circumstances to strengthen others (see James 1:2–4). We say God is good, and indeed he is better than our understanding of what good really is.

Revive Your Works

I will expose your righteousness and your works, and they will not benefit you.

—Isaiah 57:12

One of the biggest challenges to the Spirit of Christ these days is the idea that practical work satisfies Christ's demands for holiness, but that concept is not found in the New Testament. This concept comes from the world's system of rewarding hard, practical labor with material wealth and recognition, and the body of Christ has allowed that to be taught or implied in the teaching of Jesus Christ. The church has lost its savor.

Many teachers have brought this concept into the church as manifested holiness. But the Word of God will not be mocked. Be not vain or ignorant in your perception of Jesus Christ, for if your view of God is complete in your works, then your labor will not be in vain. Who we are in our deepest souls is what is most important; the works of holiness will follow.

> Make every effort to enter through the narrow door, because many, I tell you, will try to enter and will not be able to.
>
> —Luke 13:24

The saint faces two challenges of enormous proportion: the enormity of doing things godly or the enormity of doing things ungodly. Both bring enormous eternal consequences, and both involve serving a god. But that is where the similarity ends.

Doing things with the mind of Christ envelops the Christian in godly love, godly adoration, godly protection, and eternal life in the presence of almighty God. Doing things the devil's way may bring a simulated, temporary type of happiness, but the end is eternal damnation and death, quite possibly both physical and spiritual.

The Christian life is gloriously difficult, but the difficulty of it should not make us faint and fall away but challenge us to be overcomers and victors instead of victims. We can move from Satan's path to victory over life's trials. God saves humanity by his sovereign grace through the atonement of Jesus. Once we start based on his redemption to do what he commands, we find we can get it done. It's good he gives us hard things to do! If we're not continually challenged, we tend to fall away and become no earthly good for the kingdom. Just step out and make the first step, and you'll see you can do it by his grace.

Can He Trust You in Your Downtime?

Rise up.

—Joshua 8:7

One of the first lessons learned by a soldier in training is to be ready to arise instantaneously for battle. At times there is no leader to arise first. In the army of the Lord, the soldier must know that immediately when he rises, help is there. Not en route, for it was there all the time.

> "He saw that the hillside around Elisha was filled with horses and chariots of fire"

(2 Kings 6:17).

If you're called to preach the gospel, be careful during your "down" time that you don't miss what God is attempting to show you while you're away from the demands of preaching.

Can God trust you in your downtime? Can He trust you to discern the times and the seasons? Every God-given task is assigned you just for that season, and then it's time to move on.

Be careful you don't allow your investment in God's work to become a personal goal and not the vision of Jesus Christ. Can he trust you in your downtime to listen to what the Spirit of the Lord is saying, and to glorify him in your obedience? Rise up and know that the instant you move forward, your help is there and was there all the time.

> So, if you think you are standing firm, be careful that you don't fall!
>
> —1 Corinthians 10:12

The goodness of God manifested in the everyday, mundane things of life can make individuals apt to become too relaxed in Zion and, ultimately, to become no earthly good. We have lost our savor (Matthew 5:13) and are of no earthly good as soldiers of the Lord. The favor of almighty God is cherished by many, but the price of holiness is above what most are willing to pay. The consequences of disobedience will eventually come to roost. Never take for granted the goodness and grace of God, for both are contingent on the obedience of the followers of Jesus Christ.

Obedience is better than sacrifice, for we will reap the best that God has to offer and, ultimately, eternal life. Hold on to your faith. Fight the good fight, always abounding, looking beyond what is visible to see your goal in the spiritual realm. Even during the race, when all strength is gone, God will supply all the stamina you need to finish your course.

Seeing Him as He Is

Neither height nor depth, nor anything else in all creation, will be able to separate us from the love of God that is in Christ Jesus our Lord.

—Romans 8:39

The perfect love of God for me in Christ Jesus, as a spiritual human created in his image, can best be described in my mind as *evolving* into a greater and deeper understanding of God's perfect love for me. The perfect love of God for me has always been in the mind of God, but my comprehension of the depth of his love is only now becoming crystal clear in my mind.

Example: We are now going through a period of demolition. In morals, in social life, in politics, in medicine, and in religion there is a universal upturning of foundations. But the day of reconstruction seems to be looming, and now the grand question is: Are there any sure and universal principles that will evolve into a harmonious system in which we can all agree? My answer is a resounding *Yes!* My response should be to give back to God this love for me in the form of persistent praise in godly acting, speaking, giving, and praying.

> Look to the LORD and his strength; seek his
> face always.

—1 Chronicles 16:11

This verse is speaking about looking to the Lord for strength and always seeking his guidance. In the minds and ways of many this is a marvelous way of living, and for them there is no other way. Living the life of the saint is a lifestyle based on a godly attitude accompanied by a victor's mentality.

Looking intently on the face of Jesus requires a dogged attitude and a made-up mind that is not manifested in works alone but in the mind of Christ: "Let this mind be in you, which was also in Christ Jesus" (Philippians 2:5 KJV). When you arose this morning, what were you looking for? Were you looking for him as Christ the provider of all your needs as you sought to please him in praise and admiration? Or were you looking intently on his face to supply some of your needs under certain conditions at certain times?

What are you looking to him for, or are you looking to him at all? For instance, you prayed for a raise in pay but only if it comes without any demands by him that you give him constant praise and adoration. Or you want the raise without the demand that you forgive your supervisor for his last unfair evaluation. Spiritual leakage is a slow but destructive attitude that gives birth to many spiritual strongholds that can cripple for life. Once you've begun nurturing these attitudes, you'll evolve into a steep moral decline.

Look intently on the face of Jesus with a renewed, made-up mind, expecting victory regardless of the circumstances. You will then find you're not fighting a battle alone but with supernatural help from your creator, the only living God.

He who ponders a matter invites failure, but a decisive mind breeds success. Disappointment is the companion of things taken for granted.

Your longevity is enhanced by knowing those who labor among you. Drama takes center stage during idle women.

The afterthoughts of God are greater than the forethoughts of all great men. Human freedom of choice may well be the avenue to human destruction.

Songs of joy can sometimes foretell the death of a saint.

Songs of praise from a repentant heart can bring joy untold to a troubled mind. The presence of almighty God is manifested in the wings of a bird in flight.

Speak, LORD.

—1 Samuel 3:9

In our hours on the mount and in the valleys of combat, we often pray, "Speak, Lord." Being servants of the most high God, we are no strangers to prayer, for it is the only way we can effectively communicate with our heavenly Father. Then when he speaks, it is usually in a voice we are unprepared to hear. He does not speak in a vocally loud sound that arouses the sensitivity of the ears, but in circumstances in which we find ourselves enmeshed. God must destroy our determined will to understand the whys and outcomes of our circumstances based on our own interpretation of God's will for us. "That was not supposed to happen this way." "I was scheduled for this and that." "I'm under attack from the enemy." "Why, God, did you allow this to happen to me, a most favored son of the gospel?"

Am I persecuting Jesus by my overzealous preaching and evangelizing the gospel of Jesus Christ? Am I evangelizing using my own creed or the creed of another? Has my focus become diluted in pursuing another view in the name of Jesus? I have become lost in my works for the Lord without his divine involvement, so he must shout to get my attention through circumstances. I may feel I have done my duty, but have I injured him in the process?

Speak Thou to Me, O Lord

… a still small voice.

—1 Kings 19:12 (KJV)

My God speaks not to me in a loud voice nor in a whirlwind, nor in an earthquake, but in that still, small voice that quiets a troubled mind. For victory is not typically in an overwhelming deluge but small streams of joy and peace in the presence of almighty God. Strengthen me, O Lord, amid troubled waters. Lift me over and above the billowing gales of your fierce anger. Hold me in your grasp lest I fall and perish among thorns. My eyes are sore from crying and my nerves shot with fear, but you, O God, are my ever-present bastion in the middle of the storm, and I will praise you still.

... that you should follow in his steps.

—1 Peter 2:21

People are known not so much by what they say in their religion but what they do in common, mundane, everyday matters: in the grocery market checkout line, in a backed-up traffic jam when cut off by an irate driver, when confronted by an out-of-control ex–church member. Our worth is revealed in our attitude to ordinary things over which we have no control or influence when no other human being is present.

It is very difficult to get into step with God because our personality is always present to lead us down a path of familiarity away from steps leading upward to a place of the extraordinary, above those things that so easily beset us. But when we're in stride with Jesus Christ it is the easiest thing in the world, because we walk in lockstep with him in his power and might.

He has different ways of doing things, and we must be trained and disciplined to see, think, and do things his way.

That is where the difficulty comes in. Once we allow him to lead and we see things his way, we will begin to stride with him; and following becomes as easy as breathing, for we breathe without consciously trying.

The Spirit of God alters the environment in which we strive to walk with him, and that means nothing less than being in union with him. Don't give up because you find him outstepping you when you first begin the process; he always will. But his grace is enough to make up the difference. And when you walk in his steps, you will find you have a different point of view and your vision becomes as clear as crystal.

> Trust in the LORD with all your heart and
> lean not on your own understanding.
>
> —Proverbs 3:5

One of the snares facing saints is the temptation to follow that with which they are most familiar: past experiences, scholastic achievements, advice from friends and family members—and there lies the snare! What is a human beyond a pile of dust with a brain? "He breathed into his nostrils the breath of life; and man became a living soul."

Beyond this point in human existence, we become the sum of what we have learned from experience, heard, or been taught by another creature of the same origin. So what do we understand? Where is the origin of our understanding except it come from almighty God? The understanding of humans is fraught with dangers far beyond our understanding even though we may contemplate the outcome of our doings. We are unwise in that we will often follow that which is demonstrably destructive.

God advises humanity to avoid this mistake, for even our curiosities often lead to erroneous understandings—beliefs that are wrong and unacceptable before almighty God, for our understanding is not based on his truth. It is based on our rebellious desire to leave God completely out of our lives.

> Be ever hearing, but never understanding;
> be ever seeing, but never perceiving.
>
> They are darkened in their understanding
> and separated from the life of God.
>
> It sprang up quickly, because the soil was
> shallow.
>
> —Mark 4:5 (NIV)

Be careful in preaching and teaching so that you don't come off appearing pious, self-righteous, deep, or profound. The marvelous thing about the life of the saint is always the ability to see God in everything and as visible to all who will seek him. Any other view risks piety as based on a narrow view of who God is and what he is capable of being in the hearts of humanity. God is found in everyday life and activities, and his manifestation is everywhere his creation is and in all things he created.

Jesus did not say that the shallow ground would never produce a crop because it did, but when the heat of the day came, it failed because it was not rooted and grounded. However, Jesus didn't say that that ground was useless and would never produce a harvest. Every creation has a starting point, and much of it begins in shallow ground where the Spirit of God nourishes and encourages it to reach beyond shadowed ground where there is more and brighter light. God is in the shallow places if you seek him.

The Church in Court

A secular court of law is no place for Christian church leaders to settle a dispute.

—1 Corinthians 6:1, 6–8

The Dominated Mind

Let the mind of Christ richly abide in you and dominate your every waking moment in time, for this is your time as time relates to the human species. Time will not always manifest in the conscious mind, neither was it intended to do so. Time is God's guiding light for us because everyone needs a point of reference by which to do godly things in everyday affairs. It is not the big, monumental events that tax human minds but the everyday, mundane things that so easily beset us. The mind of Christ will guide us to where we need to go, and the Father will be well pleased.

> An inheritance quickly gained at the beginning will not be blessed at the end.
>
> —Proverbs 20:21

One of the challenges the Disciples of Christ must beware of is making vows as some habitually do, especially during New Year's celebrations. New Year's vows are plentiful but often not practical or possible to fulfill. Vows based on emotions are nothing but sentimental dream weaving based on unreasonable expectations. They are often composed of a long-held wish or desire for something not attainable. Vows are often made on New Year's because someone else is doing so; it is considered popular. There are several things to be mindful of when making vows, especially by the redeemed of the Lord. Vows to get rich without hard work or sacrifice usually do not mature and, if they come to pass, do not last.

Psalm 127:1 (NIV 1984) says, "Unless the Lord builds the house, its builders labor in vain." Except the Lord prepare you a mate, except you seek the advice of God and await his answer, your efforts are in vain. Be very careful what you vow, and when you do, keep that vow.

An inheritance may be gained by speculation: by random hits, the lotto, gambling of various sorts—not in the fair and progressive way of commerce, in which money has its natural increase. All such inheritances are short-lived; God's blessings are not on them, because they are not the products of industry, and they lead to idleness, pride, fraud, and knavery. A speculation in trade is a public nuisance and a curse. How many honest men have such ruined? Seek the guidance and provision of the living God in your own situation.

Seven things to consider when making vows you intend to keep:

1. Am I willing to make a required sacrifice to cause the vow to materialize?

2. Is the vow doable?

3. Is the vow practical?

4. Have I sought divine guidance?

5. What is my goal or aim in vowing?

6. Are there any kinds of resources required?

7. Can my progress be measured?

If you can honestly answer yes to all these questions, wait for a week or a month perhaps, and if the Spirit of peace has checked and approved it, go ahead.

> Strive to enter in at the strait gate: for many,
> I say unto you, will seek to enter in, and shall
> not be able.
>
> —Luke 13:24

He did not say enter in by my own interpretation of his words or enter in on the strength of a family member's relationship with him or through a denominational creed. No, we must enter in through him, Jesus Christ, who was sent by his Father, born of a woman for that specific purpose: an entranceway from sin into eternal life.

We strive and labor to overcome biases of our own and those of others and their personal agendas. Also, we often perceive a "better" and "shorter" way of avoiding trials and tribulations meant just for us individually. We fail to recognize that they strengthen our faith. What we endure is not in vain but for our own good, so we can be broken bread and poured-out wine fit for the Master's table.

Many have found out in this present time that personal concepts of holiness and righteousness will not suffice during these times of strife. When the Spirit of peace is not present, confusion, anger, deceit, anxiety, pride, and loneliness reign; even our families are often in turmoil. Our finances are in disarray, and it appears that no matter how much we apply sound discipline in spending, nothing changes.

> We have peace with God through our Lord Jesus Christ. (Romans 5:1)

> I tell you the truth, no one can enter the kingdom of God unless he is born of water and the Spirit. Flesh gives birth to flesh, but

the Spirit gives birth to spirit. (John 3:5–6 NIV 1984)

He reveals deep and hidden things; he knows what lies in darkness, and light dwells with him.

—Daniel 2:22

In the life of a believer, there are many things that will bring spiritual leakage and gradually kill one's walk in Christ if not acknowledged before God. Dogged determination must master the weak will. The agonizing unhappiness that exists in many marital relationships can continue doing a disservice to the Spirit of Christ by the refusal of one or both to confront this hidden enemy in their spirit.

My spirit is aware of this gnawing and ever-present pain in my life, but my conscious mind, bolstered by fear of the unknown, keeps me held hostage by this mistrust toward God to lead me by his divine Spirit to a godly resolution of this marital rift. God has revealed this thing to my conscious mind, long hidden in darkness. It is a mistrust of God to bring resolution.

The light of God has made me come face to face with this thing, and the light of God will resolve it if given the chance by faith in the promises of almighty God: "Is anything too hard for the LORD?" (Genesis 18:14).

Young pastors or leaders, be free of a wife hardened by fears of known origins and the glares of other women.

Otherwise the heart may be hardened by suspicion and unfounded accusations of infidelities perpetrated by jealousy and all sorts of drama borne by busybodies who thrive on the wiles of Satan.

> A sound heart is the life of the flesh: but
> envy the rottenness of the bones.

—Proverbs 14:30

A healthy, stress-free heart circulating a rich, red stream of blood is the primary cause, in the hands of God, of a healthy, long life. If the heart is overly stressed by chemical additives, negative attitudes, etc., life will be negatively impacted and quite possibly shortened. The various health and mental ailment specialists all support a healthy lifestyle consisting of eating certain foods and avoiding others. My own care provider strongly suggests I avoid stressors and anything that may cause undue stress.

But in listening to all or most of the many media health care specialists, I have never heard even one suggest that there is a spiritual component involved in healthy living that can quite possibly lead to a longer life span. As an owner's manual is to the safe operation and longevity of my sports car, so is diligent searching for the healing wisdom contained in the Holy Bible to my health. Combined with fervent, expectant prayer, this is the road map to understanding the correlation between spirituality and healthy living.

My prayer: "Lord God, I thank you for this opportunity to share these few words of encouragement to so many of your people. I pray tonight that those who have been diagnosed as having heart problems will listen to your words as the Creator of every man, woman, and child and that they, because of their faith, shall be healed."

Give glory to the LORD your God

before he brings the darkness,

before your feet stumble.

—Jeremiah 13:16

The snare in following the vision God has shown me is the lure of sin in my mortal body. The instant that vision is revealed to me, my carnal nature brings my attention to the need in my flesh to have the vision recognized and affirmed by others.

The need for recognition by others is an ongoing battle for some workers, for it quickly affirms publicly what God is doing or going to do privately in our lives. Then the Spirit of peace no longer witnesses, and vision is no longer seen as up close and personal but remote and generic, and our zeal wanes. Sometimes that need is manifested in other areas of our lives. Then we wonder why the vision is alive in our minds and in our witness but is fast becoming a distant thunder: loud but afar off.

Beware of the lure of your natural inclination to sin in small, subtle ways, because if it is not acknowledged and quickly brought before God, those infractions will no longer appear as sin but as a personal entitlement, and sin will no longer be a reality to you. "Beware the little foxes."

> There was evening, and there was morning—
> the first day.
>
> —Genesis 1:5

In the natural life the first is always the choicest and most expensive. The most expensive also requires more of a sacrifice on the part of most. It is desired by all, but many are unwilling to go the last mile to obtain the very best. In the end the best costs more to obtain. So it is in the spiritual realm. Our Father demands the first we have, for our best is found in the first, not the second or the third. He demands the first place because he has set aside in heavenly places the very best for those who sacrificed to attain the best he has to offer. From the sacrifice of praise comes worship and true fellowship in the spiritual realm.

> Then comes the culmination of all our sacrifices: "Behold, I am coming soon! My reward is with me, and I will give to everyone according to what he has done" (Revelation 22:12 NIV 1984).

Never agree with the one who complains that the best is harder to attain and necessarily more labor intensive. To attain the best God has to offer requires absolute detachment from the ordinary and a focus on the extraordinary in heavenly places. The labor is in the mind, a matter of the will, not in the grasp by human hands.

> It will not be you speaking, but the Spirit of
> your Father speaking through you.
>
> —Matthew 10:20

One of the problems I face in being obedient to what the Lord is saying to me is expecting him to speak in some startling, eerie-sounding way. But God never speaks to me in this fashion. He speaks in ways that are familiar to me so there's no excuse for my disobedience to what he tells me. I have learned to say, "Speak, Lord" (1 Samuel 3:9), and my life has become more meaningful in many ways because now, my focus is being obedient to his voice.

Shall I tell my "Eli" what God has shown me? That is where obedience presents a challenge to my walk in Christ. Sometimes we're tempted to share with those closest to us the vision God has shown or placed within our spirits. But you will have to learn to listen to the Spirit of God to guide you. And never ask the advice of others about anything God has placed before you because, if you do, you will often come down on the side of self or Satan.

The Snare in Being Right

There is a way that seems right to a man, but in the end, it leads to death.

—Proverbs 14:12

The big snare in *being right* is that it stands in opposition to being *rightly related* to him who is righteous. In my mind, all things are justified while my body satisfies its carnal craving for everything immediately. Being right satisfies the carnal ego and its need for constant and immediate gratification, and my "right to myself" justifies this self-image. However, being rightly related to Jesus Christ effectively makes me aware that a godly relationship based on being rightly related to him is far better than *being right* or standing alone in self-righteousness. Never compare individual righteousness with being rightly related to Jesus Christ, for one cannot exist with the other.

"No one can serve two masters. For you will hate one and love the other; or be devoted to one and despise the other" (Matthew 6:24).

I have spoken to you of earthly things and you do not believe; how then will you believe if I speak of heavenly things?

—John 3:12

The words of Jesus are life, health, joy, and the key to a sound mind. The Son of God, Son of man, and almighty God was manifested in the flesh to bring good news of redemption to a world devoid of the righteousness of almighty God. Oh, how we miss the greatest opportunity humans will ever be confronted with when we refuse to acknowledge the deity of Jesus Christ.

The challenge for the worker is sharing the Word of God with those who would dethrone the Son of God in favor of their own understanding of the ways of almighty God. Beware of casting the jewels of God before swine ("Give not that which is holy unto the dogs, neither cast ye your pearls before swine"—Matthew 7:6 KJV). "He who has the Son has life; he who does not have the Son of God does not have life" (1 John 5:12 NIV 1984). Beware also of allowing Satan to make you afraid of sharing the good news of redemption for all, for where sin abounds, grace much more abounds.

> Is not the whole land before you? Let's part company. If you go to the left, I'll go to the right; if you go to the right, I'll go to the left.
>
> —Genesis 13:9

*As soon as you begin to live the life of faith in God, fascinating and luxurious things will come your way. Prospects will open to you that have never opened before. These things are yours by right. You have a constitutional right to select all or most of these goodies. But if you're living the life of faith in God, you'll exercise your right to waive your rights and let God choose for you. God sometimes allows us into a place of testing where our own welfare would be a right and proper thing to consider if we were not living the life of faith in God. But we will joyfully waive our right and leave God to choose for us. This is the discipline by means of which the natural is transformed into the spiritual by obedience to the voice of God.

Whenever what you consider *right* is made the guidance in your life, it will blunt the spiritual insight. The greatest enemy of the life of faith in God is not sin but the good which is not good enough. The good is always the enemy of the best. It would seem the wisest thing in the world for Abraham to have chosen the best land for himself because that was his right, and the people around him would consider him a fool for not choosing it. Many of us do not go in Christ because we prefer to choose what is right instead of relying on God to choose for us. We must learn to walk according to the standard which has its eye on God. Aside from that, there is no other way. Let God choose for you. In everything acknowledge him, and he will direct your path.

> You have persevered and endured hardship
> for my name, and have not grown weary.
>
> —Revelation 2:3

The life of a saint is destined for trouble and upheaval, often of cataclysmic proportions; and it will seem at times of tremendous stress that there is no one to whom one may turn for consolation or even the smallest bit of sympathy. No respite in sight.

We often forget during times of extreme suffering that preparation precedes blessing (1 Peter 1:7). I have suffered many times in great and excruciating pain, yet never did I feel deserted because, in every instance, my suffering preceded blessings never previously expected. And as I look back over the times of suffering, I can detect in some small measure growth in the spiritual realm. My suffering was not in vain.

Lord, help me to know my living is not in vain, but my love for you, Oh!

The "You" beneath the Waves

Dare to discover the inner you—the "you" that resides far beneath the consciousness with which you are so accustomed to dealing in your normal everyday affairs. There is a "you" that is clamoring to be free of customs, traditions, and habits you've picked up along life's journeys up to this point. The challenge I put before you right now is intensely doable. However, it requires intense, concentrated effort to see where you need to be that will guide you to your rightful place in God.

Your rightful place in God is for you personally, and only you can find the path to this divine destination in eternity. This place is not physical but eternal in spiritual realms, attainable only to those who dare to seek that which is not ordinarily found in the usual, casual, familiar places. That is why many humans never find the key to their "assigned" place in spiritual realms.

> Elijah went up by a whirlwind into heaven.
> And Elisha … saw him no more.

> —2 Kings 2:11–12

It is not wrong for you to depend on your "Elijah" for as long as God gives him to you. But remember that the time will come when he must leave and will no longer be your guide and your leader, because God does not intend for him to stay. Even that thought causes you to say, "I cannot continue without my 'Elijah.'" Yet God says you must.

Alone at your "Jordan" (2 Kings 2:4): The Jordan River represents the type of separation where you have no fellowship with anyone else, and where no one else can take your responsibility from you. You now must put to the test what you learned when you were with your "Elijah." You have been to the Jordan repeatedly with Elijah, but now you are facing it alone. There is no use in saying that you cannot go; the experience is here, and you must go. If you truly want to know whether God is the God your faith believes him to be, then go through your "Jordan" alone.

Alone at your "Jericho" (2:15): Jericho represents the place where you have seen your "Elijah" do great things. Yet when you come alone to your "Jericho," you have a strong reluctance to take the initiative and trust in God, wanting instead for someone else to take it for you. But if you remain true to what you learned while with your "Elijah," you will receive a sign, as Elisha did, that God is with you.

Alone at your "Bethel" (2:23): At your "Bethel" you will find yourself at your wits' end but at the beginning of God's wisdom. When you come to your wits' end and feel inclined to panic—don't! Stand true to God, and he will bring out his truth in a way that will make your life an expression of worship. Put into practice what you learned while with your "Elijah"; use his mantle, and pray (see 2:13–14). Decide to trust in God, and do not even look for Elijah anymore.

But at your "Bethel" you might question whether God really did call you. Here at your "Bethel" your call will be put to the test. God called Jesus Christ to what seemed an absolute disaster, and Jesus called his disciples to see him put to death. By all human standards, Jesus's life was an absolute failure, but what humans called failure, God called triumph because God's purpose is never ever the same as our purpose. The call of God on our lives is just as complex and can never be understood or explained externally.

Adversities will surely come, and Jesus said, "Don't be surprised, but be of good cheer: I have overcome the world." Nothing creates resentment faster than preaching and teaching. Preaching awakens a resentment in people if your preaching conveys a need to be holy and the Holy Spirit convicts listeners, so they hate you. If we are in fellowship and oneness with God and recognize that he is taking us into his purposes, then we will no longer strive to find out what his purposes are. A Christian is someone who trusts in the knowledge and wisdom of God and not his own abilities. And he sees Elijah no more.

This Is Your Day

Today salvation has come to this house.

—Luke 19:9

What is your "today" to you? How is your "today" defining you? Every person has his "today" and is encouraged by our God to move up while it is still today.

Our today is a defining probe that helps determine where we are and where we are going. This can lead us to make choices we may never repeat. What happened to you today? Who did you meet today? What did you observe today that you had never seen before?

We make many and varied choices, some of which help us determine our destiny and can even wholly determine our future. We are admonished: "Today, if you hear his voice, do not harden your hearts" (Hebrews 3:15). Many will come face to face with their destiny today, will stand in the presence of greatness, and, because of the choices they make, will rise above their small beginnings—and many will not. Which choice will be yours, life in victory or defeat?

"Today if you hear His voice, Do not harden
your hearts." (Hebrews 4:7 NASB)

Perhaps today you are experiencing problems of global
proportions and, as it's the beginning of the week, you've
had the weekend to focus on all the negative aspects of
these problems. So many of us have forgotten or perhaps
never known that the Creator, almighty God, is on our
side. He loves, respects, values, and desires all the best for
us personally. He's saying to us, "Today, right now, don't
harden your hearts."

Every aspect of living the physical life is suffused with a
spiritual component centered on prayer. What almighty
God is suggesting (we have a choice) is prayer instead
of meditating on and agonizing in defeat over our
circumstances. A hardened heart does not pray because it
cannot pray. This is because prayer is an act of faith in God
to heal our dilemma by keeping his Word: "I will never
leave you nor forsake you" (Joshua 1:5).

I challenge you to immediately stop whatever you're doing
right now and take your problems to God in prayer. You
don't need to seek the advice of counsel because you're
headed to court.

This Too Will Pass

I saw great confusion.

—2 Samuel 18:29

There are times when there is spiritual confusion in the life of a saint. Our circumstances are orchestrated by God, so it's not a matter of whether I deserve it or not. It is a situation in which God is taking me through some circumstances that I would not ordinarily go through. He is showing me some things that I would not ordinarily see without going through confusion.

The characteristics I manifest in my immediate, everyday surroundings are indications of what I will be like in other surroundings. Many things that Jesus did were the most menial and commonplace things. And he signals his presence in the most commonplace, everyday things in life. It is those things and people closest to me that should inspire me most to do things God's way. "I have given you an example, that ye should do as I have done to you" (John 13:15 KJV).

I say to myself, "Sure, I'll do that when I'm in the foreign field." I'm trying to catch a horse after he's out of the barn, and I will fail as surely as the sun rises. I have to run the full course with God, but some don't get past the half mile post. I can't wait to put on the whole armor of God until after I go and bury the dead. If I do not put it on now, I will not even come near being fully clothed for battle.

Till Death Do Us Part Not

For this reason a man will leave his father and mother and be united to his wife, and the two will become one flesh.

—Ephesians 5:31

Will a man remained attached to himself in selfishness, never learning to become one with his wife, united in spirit and purpose, living as God, his creator, intended? In unity they will bring forth much fruit, doing all to the glory of God in season according to divine direction in all things. There will not be unity in confusion, jealousy, or weakness in mind, body, and spirit, for the wages of sin is death, but the gift of God is eternal life in Christ Jesus. A house divided against itself will not stand. (See Romans 6:23 and Mark 3:25).

Ephesians 2:22 reads, "In him you too are being built together to become a dwelling in which God lives by his Spirit." But not in confusion, lest the devil bring reproach among you whereby the spirit of Christ is injured, making the death of Jesus of no effect. Check out John 5:39 (NIV 1984): "You diligently study the Scriptures because you think that by them you possess eternal life." Let us live as Christ, who gave himself as a ransom for us, so that we who call on the name of Jesus out of a pure heart may be free from all accusations of the devil.

Time to Move

And we have the word of the prophets made more certain, and you will do well to pay attention to it.

—2 Peter 1:19

One of the problems in living the life of a saint is falling into a fantasy of believing that when God places us in a certain position or place, it is forever, and unless he comes before us in a burning bush, we will remain there. He may advise us through many means that our season in that place is over, but whether we adhere to his advice is a different matter. We have made valued friends, established thriving businesses, or become established in a growing ministry, but our time at that place is over.

We do well to be obedient to godly directions, regardless of the method he chooses to advise us. Move quickly, and do not hesitate, for he will have gone ahead and prepared a place for you (2 Samuel 5:24). Waiting for a manifestation will always lead to siding with Satan in disbelief and doubt. Anytime we are obedient to a godly vision, the Spirit of peace will witness when the move to obey should be started.

We walk by faith and not by sight. Indeed, obedience is better than sacrifice.

Today

If my people, who are called by my name …

—2 Chronicles 7:14

All one must do during these days of turmoil and mass confusion is look at most daily news broadcasts or scan the front or middle pages of most magazines to realize that there is mass unrest everywhere. Everyone is faced with the necessity of making life-changing decisions on a daily basis, and for many; the viable options are too few. For those who profess to be Christians, there is a way that many people these days find repugnant because they still believe they determine their eventual fate, for their faith rests in their physical and academic strengths.

> However, the one God of the Bible speaks to those who still believe, in spite of all that is transpiring: "If my people, who are called by my name, will humble themselves and pray and seek my face and turn from their wicked ways, then I will hear from heaven, and I will forgive their sin and will heal their land" (2 Chronicles 7:14).

He said this to a people who, like this nation, did not follow him wholeheartedly, and he presented them with a viable option and made it abundantly clear what the consequences would be if they elected to do otherwise. It seems the very gods (love of money) that many have served, idolized, and worshipped down through the years have for most evaporated, been stolen, or by some unforeseen means evaded possession, and they are left destitute, fearful, and unstable.

It appears that, of the idols we cherish, most have either disappeared or turned away through greed, immorality, or deception and certain politicians and athletes lead the pack. So "if my people, who are called by my name, will humble themselves and pray ... I will forgive their sins and heal their land."

> He replied, 'The LORD has appointed tomorrow as a day of rest."
>
> —Exodus 16:23 (NLT)

The notion that the body needs time purposely set aside by its earthly owner to rest and be rejuvenated is totally foreign to countless millions of people. I am sure that much of the time expended on endeavors that do not allow even a reasonable person to rest is consumed in worrying about promises of things to come and in many, many cases never will. Much time is spent in the pursuit of things that have no lasting value, and not things eternal, for those things are not readily seen and consequently not worth considering.

Past experiences have shown that if a local union shop steward announced the next day as a non-workday, every member would immediately begin making plans for celebration. Even then, for many the orders for merchandise must be placed from the vicinity of the hot dog grill.

> Jesus suggested to those who would listen:
> "Don't worry about tomorrow, for tomorrow
> will bring its own worries. Today's trouble
> is enough for today" (Matthew 6:34 NLT).

Was our Lord speaking from a spirit of arrogance? No, not at all—but from a spirit of love and compassion for his created, for there is a rest for all creation.

"For the love of money is at the root of all kinds of evil." (1 Timothy 6:10, NLT 1996). The love of money is the force that drives families to extreme lengths to remain well supplied. How does one rest? Refrain from all things manual or even from every useless thought, except that of praising and giving thanks to the Creator of us all and of all we possess.

> Too Common, Common Sense We live by
> faith, not by sight.

> —2 Corinthians 5:7

One of the strongest challenges a follower of Jesus Christ faces is walking by faith, independent of all systems of support. Every time I venture out on faith, I find something in common-sense circumstances that makes a mockery of my faith. But common sense is not faith, and faith is not common sense. They are opposites: common sense is carnal and is an expression of our carnal minds.

Faith is supernatural and is a demonstration of our trust in the promises of God. I say and believe that God will supply all my needs. Then suddenly all my supplies are gone, and right away my faith is tried, not on the mount but in everyday, common-sense circumstances.

Faith must be tested, or it will turn into sentimental fluff with no spiritual value. Tests will either prove that your faith is growing or kill it. Determine to believe God, and your faith will stand the test of time, every time. The key to built-up faith is trust in Jesus Christ.

Trouble in My Members

A saintly life is full of thorns and trials of every kind,
A life that's sure to bring some pain and grieve a
    troubled mind.
I can't explain my life's perplexities or feelings that
    keep me bound
Or even be to everyone what they believe is sound.
But I'm convinced that everyone will see and
    experience some things,
And many may not understand; it's not always what it
    seems,
And even though we love our Lord, He doesn't take
    our dreams.

He knows the ways of every man, who's often so
    unclean.
The Bible is our reference book, of stories long ago
Of many, many human feats of people gone before.
There are some things we'll never know or even
    understand
Beyond the state of holiness, pertaining to a man.
The deeper things that God reveals to some but not
    to most,
They hold the key to every life and yet He loves us so.
The holy things belong to God, and that we can
    believe,
But when we think of what we are, we have no right
    to grieve.
The sin I am, I can't deny. So wretched is this soul
The desires and things that thrill my mind, were
    young but now are old.
I'm saved, and yet my mind is caught; my members
    won't obey
To do the righteous things of God. I can't give in but
    pray.

Troubles Are Not What They Seem

Do not let your heart be troubled. Trust in
God; trust also in me.

—John 14:1

A person's first inclination when faced with obstacles in life
is to despair. It is far easier to despair than to believe and
trust in the living God. There is victory in believing that
we are not alone with our problems.

My first reaction to danger is the drive to survive. Instead,
I must believe that I can survive through the power of
almighty God, but that belief is even stronger if I know that
almighty God will take care of me because I've accepted
his only Son, Jesus Christ. The problem with humanity is
that we must see how God is going to help us overcome our
dilemmas before we believe.

Every human is the sum and total of past experiences
and beliefs which are manifested in the way we face our
obstacles, so if we never knew the power of Jesus Christ as
a burden bearer, way maker, and redeemer, we are apt to
try resolving our troubles all alone. The victory is not in
what we physically see but what we believe in our hearts
and trust in our minds.

Two Passing in the Night

When they chose new gods, war came to the
city gates.

—Judges 5:8 NIV

Frequently two people meet and right away they "feel"
they're in love—soul mates, meant for each other, etc. But
in fact, they were nothing more than two people passing
in the night, going in separate directions. God never
intended for them to establish a relationship because they
were not meant for or designed for each other. They made
that choice. Consequently, the relationship is fraught with
everything hurtful and even dangerous from time to time.
They try and try to make it work, but it's only an exercise
in futility.

Fools do rush in where wise men fear to tread. And the
beat goes on.

Two Spiritualities

The tongue also is a fire, a world of evil
among the parts of the body. It corrupts the
whole person, sets the whole course of his
life on fire, and is itself set on fire by hell.

—James 3:6

Every element of Christianity has an equally attractive counterfeit, promoted by Satan to those who have not allowed the Spirit of God to fully reveal Himself in them. The tongue is the key part in verbal communications by most living creations to convey information for purposes both good and bad. With the tongue, we offer praises to God and pay tribute to the bad.

Then there is the matter of the will: will I choose to bless God and live in his favor or will I choose to bless Satan by denying the righteousness of God and, thereby, come down on the side of the devil? With my tongue, I express a full range of praises to almighty God or I can express a full range of support for the devil.

In the spiritual realm, powers coexist. The only legitimate obligation involving us is that we offer glory, honor and praises to the creator of heaven and earth, almighty God. The other power that exists in the spiritual realm, but in a less dominant role, is the side of darkness. The sole purpose of this Prince of Darkness is to seduce the human race to the side of darkness. This creature was created by Almighty God and his powers are subject to the indwelling power of every saint in Christ Jesus.

The Prince of Darkness uses the tongue as an active member of rage that has its beginning in the mind. With the mind, we create and plan our rage against another. With the tongue, we communicate that rage couched in jealousy, envy, gossip, rage and all sorts of strife.

With the tongue we also repent, pray, testify, offer up praises to Almighty God and encourage others as we are encouraged, even by God in Christ Jesus.

Wait Until Your Change Comes

If a man dies, shall he live again? All the days of my appointed time will I wait, till my change come.

—Job 14:14

All the days of my appointed time include my warfare, my servitude, my hard times, my unfair contract, my ungrateful spouse, my ungrateful children: I will endure with patience my trials: the slander, the sickness, the gossip, the darkness in my walk in the Lord, the back stabbers in my midst. Until my change comes. Exactly all my change will incur, I don't know. It will be freedom from physical pain. It will be joy in place of unbearable grief. And I know in whom I believe.

I've been running for a long time—spring time and the buds on the limbs are coming to life. Summertime and the weather is hot and balmy. Fall comes, when the leaves are gold in color and reflect the sunlight of the ever-present God. Then here's December and the year is almost gone. The sun is going down and my winter is almost come. My change is coming; I can see clearly now; the rain is gone. All my bad feelings have disappeared; gone are the dark clouds that had me blind.

My change has come.

> "Come unto me, all ye that labor and
> are heavy laden, and I will give you rest."
> (Matthew 11:28)

Waiting for the Lord

But those who wait on the LORD Shall renew
their strength.

—Isaiah 40:31

When you be inclined to move and the Spirit of peace does
not witness, you must gather up a strong determination to
remain fixed where you are. If your inclination is that of
the Lord, the Spirit of peace will witness at the appropriate
time, and if it is a product of your own wishes, waiting will
affirm your determination to be obedient to the will of
the Lord.

Waiting for divine guidance will fortify your determination
to do God's will while learning patience in waiting on the
Lord and discipline to control the emotions.

Will you wait on the Lord? Can he trust you in the silence of
waiting for his appearing, or will you allow your misplaced
zeal to move you to a place of darkness where you have
never been before? Without the accompanying Holy Spirit,
your move will not be ordained of the Lord, and peace will
not be evident.

Those who wait on the Lord shall be renewed, and at a time determined by him the destination will become crystal clear.

Wait on the Lord

Let integrity and uprightness preserve me,
For I wait for You.

—Psalm 25:21 (NKJV)

In today's cultures, waiting is typically not something most people admire or adhere to. Instant gratification is the norm, and anything less is frowned upon; very few embrace waiting, even among those who profess to be followers of Jesus Christ.

Our Lord has taught us by his word, his example, and through his prophets the value of waiting for the fulfillment of his promises to us who are his. For those who will not accept the divinity of Jesus Christ, there is only a waiting for the wrath of God. As impatient as many are, waiting is a reality with which we all must contend. Whether one is waiting for the blessings of God on one's life or the wrath of God for sin, everyone must wait for the hand of God to move, either for or against them.

What are you waiting for?
They let the boys live.

—Exodus 1:17

What do courageous people do? First off, these women did not allow what God had entrusted to them to be destroyed by those with a different point of view. As a mother guards her unborn fetus, we must guard that which God has impregnated us with and not allow it to be contaminated or in any way harmed. May we use force to guard our unborn fetuses? Well, some things must be preserved violently.

Remember what you were saved for: that the Son of God may be manifested in you. You can't do anything to earn your salvation, but you can do everything to manifest it—not for your son, mother, father, daughter, or coworker but for the manifestation of Jesus Christ in you. That is your goal in life!

> Lord, give me understanding.
>
> —Psalm 119:169

God desires that you seek a closer relationship with him because of your love for him and his redemption; I am so thankful. Am I seeking a relationship with him because of his gifts and my desire to be some great one for the cause of Jesus Christ? He wants you to get to know him intimately, a close moral relationship that will last an eternity. The relationship should not be based on receiving his gifts or identifying with him by name only and not in spirit, but we must be one with him in attitude and walk. Identifying with Jesus Christ in name and by deed and attitude will set you apart from the world, and you will become known by the indwelling Spirit of God manifested in a defenseless, abandoned life—poured-out wine and broken bread.

Are you seeking great things for yourself? "O Lord, baptize me with the Holy Spirit." You must willfully give up your right to yourself for his right to choose for you. If not, it is because you are not abandoned fully to him; there is something you will not do or turn loose. Something you are adamantly holding on to, and the final result is often disillusionment.

He is not concerned about making you happy and blessed right now. He has concerns about your ultimate perfection in him, not your view of perfection in your current dilemma. It is your storm; go through it, and see the salvation of the Lord for yourself indeed.

> He has told us that you always have pleasant memories of us and that you long to see us.
>
> —1 Thessalonians 3:6

Most of us have many memories of things in our lives, some things in the distant past and some as recent as yesterday. But most likely amid all of them, distant and most recent, are memories fixed in our minds because of the involvement of cherished loved ones or devastating events that are so different from ordinary events that we hold on to them. In some cases, we fondly revisit them from time to time, especially during times of extreme stress, fear, anger, special holidays, etc. Then there are the memories of dire circumstances involving danger, loss of life, threats of harm, or loss of a loved one due to sickness or tragedy.

I remember my first day and night in a military barracks after arriving at Fort Jackson, South Carolina, as a recruit. I remember quite vividly cradling the head of my dad as he departed this earth early one morning. Then I remember being baptized "in the name of Jesus for the remission of [my] sins" (Acts 2:38).

I remember that God's grace shielded me through many nights, days, months, and years and assured my survival despite threats and mortal dangers of various sorts, places, and times. I remember being greatly offended at the mere mention of my need of a Savior greater than my expert military and law enforcement training. These things I remember, and these things I won't ever forget as my testimony to the power of almighty God, to the glory of God, and the Spirit of God residing in me.

What do you remember?

> Be kind and compassionate to one another.
>
> —Ephesians 4:32

Beware that you don't, in your compassion for another, allow your concern to lead you into an emotional state driven by your sentimentality. You might say, "I can't stand to see him suffer, and I've just got to do something to ease the pain," and God asks, "What is it to you?"

My compassion toward my brother in his crisis should encourage me to wrestle before God for him in prayer. Never wrestle with God in anything or you'll be the loser every time. You must learn to wrestle as Jacob did.

The chastisement of almighty God can manifest itself in many and various ways at many times and for as long as he deems appropriate.

> Then I asked, "Who are you, Lord?"
>
> "I am Jesus, whom you are persecuting," the Lord replied.
>
> —Acts 26:15

God often speaks to me with a strong hand, and when he does, he comes with all understanding of me: my past, present, goals, and intentions. When he speaks this way, there is no "wiggle" room for compromise, and "I will obey presently" is not an option. All excuses have already been dealt with.

My journey lies immediately ahead, and woe unto me if I should turn from the mission or stray off course, for I must go to and cross over Jordan.

There are times when we try to serve God with a spirit that is not his own, and we wound his Spirit by our betrayal. Thus, we give the devil what rightly belongs to God. So why must we persecute the King of glory?

We have just testified of his goodness, his sacrificial death, his redemption, and how he saved us from the misery of eternal damnation. We celebrate his birthday, we witness his manifested presence in our lives, and yet we thrust him through the heart.

Maybe I persecute Jesus by being determined to serve him in my own ways, in my own times, and in a place of my choosing. Maybe I persecute him by being a part-time servant while living in the midst of a part-time group I call friends.

> Wisdom is supreme; therefore, get wisdom.
>
> Though it cost all you have, get understanding.
>
> —Proverbs 4:7 (NIV)

Contrary to what many believe, the key to spiritual understanding is not intellect or even common sense but obedience. If I want scientific knowledge, intellectual curiosity is the key and will guide me to the necessary studies. But if I want to understand what Jesus is teaching, I will never get it unless I'm obedient.

If the things I'm striving to learn of him are dark and confusing, it is because I am stubbornly refusing to let go of something that I need to relinquish. There is something I won't do. Intellectual darkness comes from ignorance. Spiritual darkness comes from disobedience. I will never receive a word from God without immediately being tested in that thing. I disobey God and then wonder why I'm not growing in Christ. When Jesus brings a thing to me via his word, my key to growth is immediate obedience, or else my growth will immediately stop because I am in darkness.

> Wisdom is the principal thing; therefore get wisdom: and with all thy getting get understanding.

> —Proverbs 4:7 (KJV)

I am at my wits' end trying to understand the ways of this world, but wise counsel made me know that only certain things and not all things are necessary for living a successful, healthy life in this world. I know and understand many things, but because of my disposition and intimate relationship with the living God, it is best I not investigate many things. For in my "getting," a certain curiosity must exist in me to understand a thing.

Wisdom speaks through wise counsel and has shown me that many things are available to an investigative mind, but not all of them are beneficial to me (see Proverbs 12:15).

Wise Nuggets

The mind of God is revealed to a man as holiness and imparted into his soul. Wisdom is limitless in breadth and scope, the essence of a secretive mind, and few possess it.

The secret to unraveling a dire dilemma is to first expose the need of the secrecy; the urgency will soon evaporate, revealing the truth of a matter.

A publicly acknowledged secret will soon be revealed by those just as secretively, and the beat goes on.

Human drama demands attention from others, and the drama feeds on itself to meet the need for drama of those who seek drama, and the beat goes on.

The heart of the comedian is filled with a desire to avoid and disallow some of life's inevitable experiences and consequences of past hurts.

Personal anger can be a flaw along one's path to perfection but can slow down one's path to destruction if directed at self-improvement. So is there a contradiction?

Woe Is Me

Anyone who claims to be in the light but hates his brother is still in the darkness.

—1 John 2:9

The snare in the saint's walk is the command of Jesus to be in the light, as he is the light; but the call of sin is continuous and often momentarily overwhelming. The minute-by-minute, hour-by-hour, day-by-day lure of sin is ever present, and only those who have abandoned all to Christ will stand.

Never allow the guilt associated with your knowledge of the spiritual in your life to stifle your growth in Christ. Your need of salvation was foreordained long before your existence, and God's Son, Jesus, was sent here to make a way of escape for you so that you could escape eternal punishment for your sin. In his words: "He that believeth and is baptized shall be saved; but he that believeth not shall be damned" (Mark 16:16 KJV). So don't think it strange when those thoughts of things that oppose the presence of God in your life come to mind. Do not allow the guilt *of thou shalt not* to discourage you from persevering in prayer, while seeking to know God personally. "Therefore, there is now no condemnation for those who are in Christ Jesus" (Romans 8:1).

Woe to Me

If that I may apprehend that for which also
I am apprehended.

—Philippians 3:12

There are many things we can choose to do in life and succeed; there are many professions we can pick and then practice quite successfully. However, never choose to be a full-time worker for the Lord. If he chooses you, then he himself will show you what your options are, but if you choose independently to work for him, you will ultimately fail because your life will have become a life of drudgery and will seem laborious. You will come to dislike almost everything associated with the uncompromised ministry of Jesus Christ because he will appear to demand more than you are willing to give. However; if he apprehends you, *woe to you* if you turn to the right or to the left. We are not here to work for God by choice unless we are apprehended by him to do so.

When he has called you and qualified you, there is never such a thought as "Well, I'm not qualified to do this or that," or "Why do I have to do this or that?" Some at this point easily fall into a backslidden position because the sentimental attraction to the Lord's vineyard has become a disdain, and the message of Jesus Christ will become burdensome and have no effect.

> Hope deferred makes the heart sick: but
> when the desire cometh, it is a tree of life.

—Proverbs 13:12 (KJV)

Few things in life can hurt as much as dashed expectations. During the coming Christmas season, many will suffer deferred hopes when the gifts of money and other physical tokens of affection do not appear under the Christmas tree due to lack of resources customarily available for sharing with loved ones and others.

For many, especially those who are experiencing a long period of unemployment and are heads of households with young children, these will be times of painful challenges, not ordinarily encountered. In the past, there usually was, even on the day just before Christmas, a miraculous way to provide some basic essentials, and everyone, especially the youngsters, received something from Santa.

From all indications, things will be much worse this season, and hope for many will be deferred. However, as a follower and disciple of Jesus Christ, I am perennially hopeful and encouraged by the words of my God, "All things work together for good to them that love God" (Romans 8:28).

For hundreds of years many professing Christians have proudly proclaimed, "Jesus is the reason for the season," although attitudes frequently indicated otherwise. In view of the prevailing domestic economic conditions existing in so many homes, will we or can we still proclaim, "Jesus is the reason for the season"? Because if we will, then the lack of Christmas goodies will not seem so bad after all.

Let us remember: this too will pass. For there is life after Christmas and preparations always precede blessings, and desires may eventually come to fruition. Let's just be thankful for what we do have: our health, shelter, families, and food, even though it may be meager. And if we still have a job, someone who loves us, and yes, last but by no means least, these United States of America, we must be grateful.

But Peter followed him afar off unto the high priest's palace, and went in, and sat with the servants, to see the end.

—Matthew 26:58

The matter of the will comes into play when I am faced with a decision that immediately confronts my instinct for survival or my need for affirmation from those around me.

The moment my immediate physical well-being is in doubt, I am forced to make a decision to either stand on my trust in God or abandon him for the affirmation offered. If the affirmation is offered by Satan, I am in spiritual darkness, and my perception of the will of God is diminished.

That I have been in the presence of my God is of no consequence at this point, for my natural inclination to flee and give in to my carnal needs becomes paramount. The war in my members is raging, and the light of God is also afar off. It is now a matter of the mind and the Spirit of Christ which has become second nature, for the call of my flesh is as a raging sea and will not be denied.

In my mind the flesh must be satisfied with my perceived need for physical safety or other carnal desires that oppose the laws of God. My flesh cries out for recognition, and I must recognize that carnal need before I reward my flesh with what it craves. When acknowledging the war in my members, I can either offer satisfaction by providing what is demanded or speak to and stand on the Word of God: "Man shall not live by bread alone ..."

This war is not against flesh and blood, but spiritual warfare manifested in physical, mundane, everyday events. These are spiritual forces I am not capable of defeating alone but only by the power of almighty God in Christ Jesus.

"Consider it pure joy, my brothers, whenever you face trials of many kinds" (James 1:2 NIV 1984). Temptation is the manifestation of my own thoughts and wishes, and these thoughts lead to evil actions. For the pagan, sin results finally in the death penalty from God because of their neglect of the offer of so great a salvation.

"But Lord, what about this man?"

"What is that to you?"

John 21:21–22

One of the most difficult things to learn even as disciples of Jesus Christ is to keep out of another people's business. Some have adopted the belief that being servants of God makes us our brother's keeper, according to the Bible's reference to a universal brotherhood.

We see a coworker in Christ in the midst of trying circumstances, and immediately our response is "I cannot bear to see him suffer such agony; I must relieve him of his pain." God asks, "What is it to you? Who made you your own providence?"

Who made you to know God's order for another's life? If you are going through a spiritual quagmire and the Spirit of peace is not present, quite possibly it is because you have been interfering in someone's life. Do not let it go on, but immediately seek out the problem.

We are tempted to barge in and correct every Christian for each perceived fault. But is God prompting you, and have you earned the right to rebuke that one? If you are asked to give advice, be sure you are rightly related to Christ before you proceed, and if so, the Spirit of God will advise through you with direct discernment. If you are rightly related to him all the time, discernment will come through you to bless another soul. Be sure you are rightly related to Christ, or your carnal spirit will fill the space normally filled by the Holy Spirit, and confusion will reign.

Most people live on the edge of self-consciousness—consciously serving and obeying God for the recognition. We are to serve God as little children: obeying unconsciously without one moment of considering what we should or should not do. When we are self-consciously pouring ourselves out as wine and broken bread, we are not there yet. If we must consciously relate to others our works for God, we are not there, but we risk seeming pious.

A saint is never consciously a saint but is consciously dependent upon God.

> You do not realize now.
>
> —John 13:7

It is truly amazing how we will know the will of God in a thing and either debate ourselves out of it or allow others to kill our knowledge of God with foolish, unlearned questions. Eventually we will fall to the side, and disobedience sets in.

Knowledge of God is a personal thing, yet we allow others to dictate our salvation or obedience based on their personal unbelief or doubt. This is spiritually deadly to those who are not sure of their own security in Christ. One must be sure beyond a shadow of a doubt where he stands and know that God is fully able to do what He has promised (Romans 4:21).

Often one can't share his vision with certain others lest they hamper that vision. It is strongly suggested that once one acknowledges a vision God has given, it is necessary that immediate, not delayed, obedience be the absolute priority. If not, one may be counseled to veer off in the wrong direction.

> For no matter how many promises God has made, they are "Yes" in Christ. And so through him the "Amen" is spoken by us to the glory of God. (2 Corinthians 1:20)

> If a man die, shall he live again? All the days of my appointed time will I wait, until my change come.

> —Job 14:14

Cast your cares on the Lord and He will sustain you; He will never let the righteous fall.

—Psalm 55:22

Jesus saith unto him, Rise, take up thy bed, and walk.

—John 5:8 (KJV)

Jesus speaks here as God. He speaks in no other name but his own, with authority that belongs to God alone. And what are the consequences? Many immediately became whole, and this sudden restoration of health and strength was incontestable proof of the power of God in Jesus Christ. It was customary for good things to follow in the wake of a miracle. The aftereffects related to some circumstance that attested to the truth of his supernatural power. Immediately after the miracle of five loaves of bread, he ordered the fragments collected, and they were greater in quantity than the original five loaves, after thousands were fed. Immediately after Jesus spoke supernatural words to the woman at the well, she rushed into town and proclaimed Jesus to everyone.

The proof is incontestable: Jesus can do abundantly above what he has promised. Take up your bed and walk! Where there is faith and hope, there is deliverance; your attitude determines your altitude in your walk as a disciple of Jesus Christ. The scriptures declare, "As a man thinketh in his heart, so is he." If he thinks in his heart he is a loser, then that's what his life will be.

Rise, take up thy bed, and walk!

Your life is hidden with Christ in God.

—Colossians 3:3

The Spirit of God witnesses to the simple almighty Spirit of God in Christ, for the two are one. It is the simple, uncontentious, humble spirit residing in Christ which is brought out in the gospel of Jesus Christ. And that Spirit resides only in those who are his. So when you receive the vision of God in Christ, you are one with him. That is an honor that many claim but some have not and will not find because they will not allow the Spirit of God in Christ to have free rein in their mortal souls. And thereby they become obstacles and stumbling blocks before God to others.

So no matter what form in which the stumbling block looms before you, it is your choice whether you accept or reject its presence in your life. If you reject its presence in your life, it cannot be an obstacle in your way, and success will always be yours as long as the Spirit of God in Christ is taking the lead, for you will have learned to cast your burdens on him, and he will see you through every time! Step over the obstacles.

> Trust in the LORD with all your heart and
> lean not on your own understanding.

—Proverbs 3:5

There are many things in both spiritual and physical realms that can be excruciatingly painful to every man, woman, and child. Pain is no respecter of persons. All pain, however, is subject to the laws of cause and effect. Many ailments, of both known and unknown origins, can be healed by specialists trained to address these ailments because of the specific training they have received in that area.

There are many ailments that are prevalent and thriving among us today during this period of physical and spiritual lack that can only be healed by the One who created all things under the sun. Regardless of the manifestation of an ailment or how the ailment makes its presence known, successful treatment must begin and end at the root cause of that ailment.

During the holiday season and quite possibly far beyond, the spirit of a man, woman, or child is apt to experience intense pain because of the shock associated with loneliness or the sudden loss of usually available goods not present today.

Nothing—no pain, no aggravation—can be compared with the bruised spirit in a man, woman, or child, and no one can effectively treat that hurt because it is of a spiritual nature and must be treated using godly spiritual principles. We must use spiritual tools designed specifically for that purpose by the Creator, Jesus Christ himself. We often find ourselves at a point in time when we meet our Waterloo. Here crucial decisions must be made that cannot be delayed, because to do so would invite more pain, aggravation, or even, in some instances, a loss of life.

Many of us, even right now, are desperate for some viable way out of our dilemma of not having enough food for our Christmas tables, toys for our tots, or at least basic foods for day-to-day living. We're at our wits' end. "So where do we go from here?" is the question. Especially with an economy gone mad, countless thousands have found themselves limping along "where the rubber meets the road." All natural resources have long since been consumed, destroyed, taken away. We may have been forced into this situation by ignorance of the part divinity plays in our lives.

The God of the Bible says; "If my people, who are called by my name, will humble themselves and pray and seek my face and turn from their wicked ways, then I will hear from heaven, and I will forgive their sin and will heal their land" (2 Chronicles 7:14). If you are where your rubber meets the road, or you've found yourself at your Waterloo (and from all appearances, most of us in this nation are struggling), then let's consider what our creator says. Without him we will not succeed. He will deliver us while in our circumstances, not out of our circumstances.

Shackled by Freedom

Now I will break their yoke from your neck
and tear your shackles away.

—Nahum 1:13

As created beings with the ability to choose, humans can do or not do many things in life. They can choose to look far into the future, even beyond what their eyes can discern, for they can see with their spiritual eyes and imagine all manner of places and circumstances. They can look far back into the distant past into places and things they should have long forgotten, but their minds, unlike that of a programmed computer, are created to date and predate ancient pieces of life.

This flesh and blood creation made in the image of their creator was destined at the point of origin to reign over all earthly creations. But because of their God-given ability to choose one thing over another, many allowed the enemy to tempt them, and they became shackled by their own inbred ability to pick one thing over another. Consequently, their mind and body became shackled for the duration of their earthly reign.

I find that this deplorable situation is like being locked behind a chain-link fence and not knowing I have the key, in that almighty God has allowed his very own creation, made in his image, to choose life or effectual suicide and has, simultaneously, given humanity the very key to their survival. But humans must choose to accept the key and open the door: "Behold, I stand at the door, and knock" (Revelation 3:20 KJV).

What does it benefit us to have knowledge of good and evil unless we choose the good and live a life that will glorify God? Many deliberately choose evil and die, which grieves the heart of God but confirms a spiritual law that says the wages of sin is death, for God cannot entertain sin. Either choice is made by those whom God created, and each choice determines our eternal destination, for it is our right to choose.

It is likewise our choice to choose wisdom and live, for the wages of sin is death but the gift of God is eternal life in Christ Jesus to the glory of God.

Yes, There Is

For everything that was written in the past was written to teach us, so that through endurance and the encouragement of the Scriptures we might have hope.

—Romans 15:4 (NIV)

During these times of abject poverty and lack of the ordinary, everyday goods we've come to depend on are hard to come by. Christmas, especially in the minds of our little ones, is presenting monumental challenges to most families. I remember years ago, as a youngster, making many trips from our small bedroom in the little modest, plain home in which I was reared in Baltimore County Projects. My father, a transplanted North Carolina farmer, was employed as a steel worker, earning an income that was considered somewhat low but adequate for our family of four.

My trips to the living room on Christmas Eve were full of childish Christmas expectations based on our hope that Santa Claus would have quietly arrived and left his customary goodies of hard candies, apples, oranges, raisins, and assorted toys. Then there came the inevitable moment when my sister and I lost that certain degree of innocence only found in youngsters who have not been exposed to the harsher realities of life when we almost magically discovered that Santa Claus was only a manifestation of the love of a devoted father and mother.

But those were days, weeks, months, and years of hope. We had a deeply held belief that Christmas would usher in a new reality that consisted of fun, excitement, and the joy of pulling my Radio Flyer red wagon around the neighborhood, basking in the admiration of my playmates. We enjoyed the camaraderie of other children as the boys played with their marbles and slingshots.

Yes, there is a "Santa Claus" if you would allow yourself to escape the rigors and heartbreaks of the realities birthed by the daily news pundits and the blaring sounds of police sirens. Santa Claus comes when you take the time to sit down and tell an exciting story to some small listening ears as you all enjoy a cup of hot chocolate. Santa Claus does not have to come with a computer or radio-controlled car or a cell phone. However, perhaps a simple hug accompanied by the words, "I love you" will suffice and bring much joy.

"For everything that was written in the past was written to teach us, so that through endurance and the encouragement of the Scriptures we might have hope."

I pray that, with all we have been through and endured both as a nation and individually, we have learned that much of what we depend on is not and was not created in a dish observed under a microscope but in an incarnated heart filled with rich, oxygenated, red blood. It was created by a mind far greater than that of a typical human; a heart filled with hope, even a hope that is far beyond any scientific comprehension: the mind of Jesus Christ. Yes, there is a "Santa Claus." If you look for him, you will find him.

This Season

If anyone loves me, he will obey my teaching.
My Father will love him, and we will come to
him and make our home with him.

—John 14:23

Life is full of trials of many sorts. Most trials challenge us to move beyond where we ordinarily reside (spiritually, emotionally) into a higher place unfamiliar to us. Some are born into circumstances where many of the physical comforts of life are already established, and the individual spiritual and emotional demands are not recognized or acknowledged in favor of maintaining an appearance of stability or well-being in the presence of material wealth.

In this life, everyone must answer to the creator of all creation, the Lord Jesus Christ (Philippians 2:10). However, the challenge to love God is not something humans ordinarily rise to because our natural inclination is to love ourselves incessantly.

As summer, fall, and winter come on in a predictable schedule, each brings predictable challenges. But almighty God prepares all creation for the coming changes in weather which present every man, woman, and child with unique trials that will often determine one's survival; spiritual and physical.

The season of Christmas celebrations brings with it new challenges for many and, for some, the same challenges faced in the past with no obvious movement beyond their present plight. Holding on to and practicing the same mode of living will often bring the same unfruitful results and for some an unhealthy lifestyle. This is not the will of almighty God, but the prince of this world has full sway. However, only those who are blind to the truth will succumb to his wiles. Choose to love God, and He will come into you with a peace that is far beyond and above a man's understanding of love, for where there is true love, there will be peace and understanding.

Now Then

Now then, listen, you wanton creature, lounging in your security and saying to yourself, "I am, and there is none besides me."

—Isaiah 47:8

We experience many inconvenient things in life that could be avoided if we would only pay attention to some small but important details. It can be disappointing to locate that hard-to-find, seldom used flashlight during a raging storm, only to learn that the chemical has slowly seeped out since it was last used.

The challenge to a saint is often an effort to avoid spiritual leakage as a result of spiritual indifference. A worker can easily adopt an attitude of indifference if not directly affected by external circumstances.

Various historical records will confirm that countless nations, cities, and individuals have been destroyed by enemies or from within. They were blinded by self-indulgence, pride, or worshipping idols. A spiritual inventory will quickly illuminate the need of a reenergized praise and worship time and place.

My spiritual growth is on the wane, and the Spirit of peace will be absent and will not be missed unless I am in a habit of effectual, fervent praying on a daily basis.

Spiritual leakage can be defined as a gradual waning of the desire to praise and worship God on a regular basis, although not necessarily at the same time all the time.

Spiritual leakage is often found in families where most members are seldom all together at once—where parents are regularly meeting each other going and coming. Where there is spiritual leakage, faith will suffer and soon be a fading memory. Fervent and invigorating conversation about godly principles has become a thing of the past and hot tempers a regular problem among formerly close family members. Prayer in the life of the saint is comparable to fuel in the operation of the automobile engine: a necessity in the smooth operation of the car.

James 5:16 says, "The effectual fervent prayer of a righteous man availeth much."

> I will pray with my spirit, but I will also pray
> with my mind; I will sing with my spirit, but

I will also sing with my mind. (1 Corinthians 14:15)

Stopping Now Is Not an Option

We do many things in life that can either prolong our lives or hasten their end. Some things are necessary in order that other things occur successfully.

Then there are things we do because of the expectations of others. But regardless of what motivates us to do even the necessary things, we often encounter a mental roadblock that says to us, "You can't do that" or "You're too tired" or "Let Joe or Janice do that."

Sometimes we are well into the project when gradually a spirit of defeat enters the mind, and the original fervor just seems to have dissipated. Sometimes these thoughts come suddenly because of something external, but the results are the same: all hope is gone.

I'm reminded of an old school gospel song titled "You can make it if you try." The lyrics run something like this: "You going to live until you die … Oh yeah, you can make it if you try." The message seems to imply: "As long as you're alive, you will be faced with obstacles, but you can make it if you try."

When I have started a project and perhaps not even gone beyond the first stage, I've gone too far to turn around.

The fact that I have even started denies me the option to stop now.

My spirit says, "You can go all the way if you but try; just try." But my mind is still saying to me, "You need to just stop." That is where I need to be led by the Spirit of God. If I will only try and not give strength to the notion of defeat or the mind-set that says I can't go on, then I will go on.

If I amputate my leg because of aches and pains before I start my journey, I will never complete my journey because I have killed all hope of success before, I have begun. In every successful venture the hardest part is overcoming the natural tendency to remain motionless. The most difficult part of moving a stalled vehicle is getting it to move. Once it is moving, there is less resistance and much less effort required.

You *can* make it if you try!

Trapped

And that they will come to their senses and escape from the trap of the devil, who has taken them captive to do his will.

—2 Timothy 2:26

The dictionary defines the words *snare* and *trap* interchangeably, and in practice they mean the same thing. A common snare in the life of a saint occurs when one chooses a mate to satisfy a perceived need for companionship, only to find that the desired qualities are not present in the one selected. This results in a feeling of being trapped or snared in a situation from which there is no apparent escape.

The situation is worsened by an inability to admit that a mistake was made in the initial selection, which becomes more evident with the passing of time. Needless to say, this relationship can promote and harbor much disharmony and breed antagonism on the part of those involved. As in other situations where there is pain and suffering, it is recommended that the root cause be examined so that the core of that problem may be "cauterized," eliminated by confession, repentance, and prayer. However, only the most devoted and abandoned workers in Christ can admit to such potentially devastating errors in judgment, and therefore many prolong the agony.

> The healing process requires the willing participation of both parties in confession: "Therefore confess your sins to each other and pray for each other so that you may be healed. The prayer of a righteous man is powerful and effective" (James 5:16).

Naturally, our emotions lead us to believe that over time the feelings of being trapped will subside and a feeling of less conflict will arise, making us happier and more content in our relationship. But if our spiritual parents did not see the need for the verse just quoted to aid our recovery, it would not be there.

> But thou, when thou prayest, enter into thy closet.

> —Matthew 6:6 (KJV)

Naturally, many things are done secretly. Not all things done secretly are necessarily bad or undesirable. Many wars, natural and spiritual, have been won or avoided due to secret negotiations between parties. All things have the potential of being done secretly or openly, depending on who is doing what and for what purpose. There is a time and a season for all things.

The life of a saint is a life fraught with dangers of every sort from every side, from those who oppose the gospel of Jesus Christ and, simultaneously, from those who emulate him.

The life of a saint is always on display to his natural surroundings, for his attention is desired by many who would know the source of his peace but are not willing to submit to the will of him who provides that peace, that is, the peace that passes all understanding.

Therefore, the saint must enter his secret closet, where all external noises clamoring for his attention are shut out. In his secret closet alone, he meets the One who sent him into his field of endeavor: the Lord's vineyard. There in his closet, the saint is strengthened and reinvigorated for the work in the vineyard.

By divine necessity, some things God has reserved in secret for certain ones whom he has set aside for certain times. Some things are so divinely constructed and purposed in life that they are only revealed at certain times under certain situations. "It is given unto you to know the mysteries of the kingdom of heaven, but to them it is not given" (Matthew 13:11 KJV).

The apostle Paul eloquently stated the following:

> My purpose is that they may be encouraged in heart and united in love, so that they may have the full riches of complete understanding, in order that they may know the mystery of God, namely, Christ. (Colossians 2:2)

This is a time when pain is no longer intense in my life. I was vividly alive under the influence of pain, which now has waned. The center of my existence is far beyond the presence of my pain. I no longer even acknowledge pain's unwelcome existence in my space. It is in my personal space after all, and pain has decided to exist in my space with me.

Pain was a constant enemy, but I have learned to accept its presence in my being, not as a thing of annoyance, not like an unwelcome visiting cousin who will not go away, but as a visitor who is present and won't go away and has no intention of ever leaving. So my pain is tolerated but not loved.

In my pain I am free. My mind is free to fly away to regions and realms far beyond my realm of existence when I am bound by physical and spiritual confines but free to rise above any confines dictated by those like me—men themselves, bound by ignorance, prejudices, and biases of all sorts and worst of all by their own inner demons. There are inner demons and external demons, but all are demons just the same.

Can it then be said that a human's pain is his friend? Perhaps so, or maybe not. Jesus was acquainted with pain, but he overcame the ravages of pain to rise to his Father. He returned to the place where his pain was greatest, but his mind was never captivated by his pain but endured.

Pain then is a slow preparation for death. Often it is slow, degrading, and insidious; it is mind boggling and can be relentless. It leads to the destination this side of eternity. It is the preparation for entrance into a man's eternal destination if eternity is his destination, in that realm beyond death. There is the death of the body, and there is the death of the spirit.

You and I are ordinary beings extraordinarily made, so rise and fly away. Fly way beyond and above your pain because this not your home unless you have made that choice.

Printed in the United States
By Bookmasters